# Issues in
# American Education

## Commentary on the
## Current Scene

Edited by
ARTHUR M. KROLL
Harvard University

OXFORD UNIVERSITY PRESS
New York   London   Toronto
1970

# Preface

Programs preparing professional personnel for services in education increasingly include among training experiences some form of systematic introduction to major issues in American education. Such experiences may be provided through courses with such titles as "Introduction to Education," "Cases and Concepts in Education," "The American School," and so on.

Such courses frequently rely upon instructor-prepared case material or draw upon available published material on current issues in education—usually issues which have multiple or ambiguous alternatives for resolution. These courses typically center upon currently emerging issues. Appropriate sources of such position statements, controversial or not, are not easily identified. To be sure, education has its journals, textbooks, and books of readings. Yet the type of material referred to here is seldom assembled in a single volume for the ideas and concepts involved are frequently in evolution or transition, and cover widely disparate topics. What few existing sources have managed to do is to present to the student or to the practitioner an account, fresh and informed but not highly technical, of problem areas that are in the mainstream or emerging at the forefront of education.

This volume assembles papers covering a diverse cross-section of issues in education. This collection emerged from the Institute for Administrators of Pupil Personnel Services of the Graduate School of Education, Harvard University, Cambridge, Massachusetts, where they were initially delivered as major addresses. These position statements stimulated such vigorous analysis and deliberation among Institute participants that an effort was initiated to share these materials with the education profession at large. The contributions are still warm; they are authoritative and readable.

Generally, the book is organized as follows: The initial papers deal with problems in values, ethics, and philosophy. These are followed by considerations of possible structural changes within education brought about by such developments as a national assessment program and the rise of collective negotiations. Several societal influences such as technology and urban integration are then explored. These are followed by discussions of the changing nature of guidance and administration. The volume concludes with an educational statesman's plea for enlightened sensitivity to the interplay of persons and organizations.

Expressions of appreciation are extended to the authors represented herein and to Theodore R. Sizer, Dean of the Harvard Graduate School of Education, for his continued interest in and support of the Institute and its publication endeavors. Special thanks go to Alice Sizer Warner and Lois W. Marshak for their editorial assistance in the production of this volume, and to Jo Anne M. Austad, Barbara A. Cullinane, and Mei Lie Wong who collectively bore the secretarial burden. It is the editor's hope that the reader may glean from the contents of this book some sensitivity for the ferment, fervor, and excitement within American education.

A.M.K.

*November 1969*
*Cambridge, Massachusetts*

# Contents

# Contributors

ARNO A. BELLACK, Professor of Education, Teachers College, Columbia University, New York, New York

JOHN F. COGSWELL, Associated Psychological Consultants, Los Angeles, California

DANA L. FARNSWORTH, M.D., Director of University Health Services and Henry K. Oliver Professor of Hygiene, Harvard University, Cambridge, Massachusetts

ANDREW W. HALPIN, Research Professor of Education, University of Georgia, Athens, Georgia

ROBERT J. HAVIGHURST, Professor of Education and Child Development, University of Chicago, Chicago, Illinois

MICHAEL H. MOSKOW, Associate Professor of Economics and Education, Director of the Bureau of Economic and Business Research, Temple University, Philadelphia, Pennsylvania

THOMAS F. PETTIGREW, Professor of Social Psychology, Harvard University, Cambridge, Massachusetts

JUERGEN SCHMANDT, Associate Director, Program on Technology and Society, Harvard University, Cambridge, Massachusetts

DONALD E. SUPER, Professor of Psychology and Education, Teachers College, Columbia University, New York, New York

ROBERT ULICH, James Bryant Conant Professor of Education, Emeritus, Harvard University, Cambridge, Massachusetts

# Issues in American Education
## Commentary on the Current Scene

# The Values of Youth

ROBERT J. HAVIGHURST

While the values of people depend upon the society in which they live, so do the growth and effectiveness of that society depend upon the values of its citizens. Today's social changes and value changes challenge the educational system to develop forms of teaching and learning and ways to use free time which will help young people become effective in a democratic, highly productive society.

The values of people depend upon the society in which they live. Caveman society and the society of an economy of abundance have values so different in relative importance and so different in the scope of human experience to which they refer that comparison is not useful.

As the social setting in which people live changes through time, the values of the people change. When social change is rapid, value change is correspondingly rapid.

The current century is one of rapid and pervasive social change for the United States. Therefore it is one of major change in values. The only values which have not changed are so inclusive or so abstract that they are at all times only vaguely defined. For instance, the values of honesty and of friendliness have not changed in their importance, though the actual theaters in which honesty and friendliness are of greatest social value have changed. Again, justice is an abstract word for a value, as is democracy. These values are as important now as they were a long time ago, but their operational meanings are different today than they were only ten years ago.

3

# I. Areas of Major Value Change

There are three areas in which events of the period 1950-1970 have produced such far-reaching changes in the lives of Americans that they can probably be called *crises* or turning points in our social history. In working through these crises we are changing our values substantially.

Young people are especially sensitive to the value changes associated with these crises. Perhaps this is because they are forming their own values during this period of change, in contrast to their elders, whose values were substantially formed in an earlier social setting. When one already has a fairly well-organized set of values by which one steers one's life, it is not easy to change these values, even though the changing social setting may make them obsolete.

Insofar as we have a barrier against communication between the generations today, it may be due to the fact that the younger is hammering out its values on the social anvil of the 1960's rather than that of the 1920's or even the 1940's.

To examine these three areas of rapid and deep social change, it is useful to compare and contrast the social setting of 1900-1920, out of which the values of the 1920's emerged, with the social setting of 1950-1970, out of which the values of the 1970's are emerging.

## A. THE OPEN SOCIETY

By this phrase we mean a society in which there is *opportunity* for the individual to make a satisfactory place for himself which fits his abilities and his motives. The notion of an open society carries with it the notion of relatively free mobility, based on effort and ability, from one social class to another. *Justice* is a term applied to the procedures for opening and keeping open the avenues of opportunity.

The term *open society* has an international political meaning, as well as a domestic socioeconomic personal meaning. The truly open society seen in terms of social groups of substantial size which occupy territory is one in which these groups or nations are politically free and abide in a state of peace and orderly cooperation with one another.

During the 1900-1920 period, the American society had a considerable degree of openness for its white members, but not for its colored members: Negroes, Orientals, and Indians. Even during this period, the socio-economic lines between manual workers and white-collar workers were more sharply drawn than they are today, except for farmers, whose children could move quite freely in the society.

The international society during this period was compartmentalized, with little exchange or cooperation between the Occident and the Orient, a large part of the human race living in colonial status, and little or no cooperation between the great religious bodies.

The 1950-1970 period is marked by major changes within the United States and in the international society. The civil rights movement has produced a realistic basis for positive action to open the society to Negroes. Orientals now move about relatively freely and successfully in search of economic opportunity. Manual workers through labor organizations have won a relatively better standard of living and are sending a much higher proportion of their children through high school and college than they did in 1900-1920.

In the area of international relations, colonial status is a thing of the past, though there continues to be a gap between the wealthy and the poor societies. Hence the nations communicate better and cooperate more effectively than ever before. The religious bodies of the world are holding ecumenical congresses, exploring and expanding their areas of common understanding and cooperation.

When there are stubborn and bitter conflicts between nations, and between political groups within nations, as in the Middle East and in Vietnam, the rest of the world becomes concerned, and the conscience of the citizenry of the United States is involved as it has never before been involved in a military undertaking of the American government.

The ideal of the open society, with justice and opportunity for all, is an active ideal for which many young people are making substantial sacrifices. Their parents and grandparents, in most cases, had very little concern with this area of human activity.

## B. THE GREAT ORGANIZATION—INDUSTRIAL, ECONOMIC, POLITICAL, AND EDUCATIONAL

Since 1950 there has been a growth in size and complexity of most of the organizations in American society. Industrial and business corporations have grown by expansion of their business and by merger with other corporations. School systems have grown enormously in size, due to the postwar increase in birth rate and also to the merger of small school districts. Universities and colleges have expanded, especially the state-supported ones. Only local government has not expanded through mergers very much, but local government agencies have proliferated as urban renewal and welfare functions have been taken on. Federal government organizations have multiplied.

The proportion of the white-collar labor force which is employed by large organizations has increased greatly, while the proportion who are self-employed or who work for organizations with ten or less employees has been reduced accordingly. The small food shop or clothing store or hardware store owned and operated by one man with two or three employees has been replaced by the supermarket and the department store chain. The small factory with one hundred employees and a corresponding office and executive staff has been bought up by a large industrial corporation. The one-man law office or the two-man partnership has been partially replaced by the large law firm. The doctor with his own office has been replaced partially by a clinic consisting of eight or ten specialists. The church with a pastor and a part-time director of religious education may have grown to have a professional staff of four to six people. The small college with fifty faculty members has grown to five hundred faculty members. Even the one-family farm has lost ground to the large mechanized industrial farm corporation.

During this period the phrase "organization man" has come into use to describe a man or woman whose work and loyalties are tied up in a complex organization. The goals of the big organization are growth, diversity, and efficiency. Success is measured in these terms. Values associated with growth, diversity, and efficiency are learned by the successful people, at the expense of values more closely associated with smaller organizations and one-man business and professional operations.

The electronic computer in its various forms has become the agent and the symbol of the organization. It keeps track of the manifold operations of a complex system by storing up more information than any human mind can hold in usable condition and by feeding this information into the controls of the system when needed.

The act of operating a complex organization successfully is one of combining the mechanical operations of a computer with a special kind of human interaction that operates rationally to make the decisions which should not be trusted to mechanical devices. The crucial question often is—what values will be maintained and what values will be sacrificed by the decisions that must be made?

During the 1900-1920 period American organizations were relatively small, whether they operated in business, government, or education. When an industrial corporation became large enough to threaten to monopolize the sale of its product, it was dissolved under the Antitrust Law. Then came mass production, mass distribution, automation, and cybernation, all aimed at efficient production of large quantities of goods. After World War II there was expansion of American business into foreign markets with the acquiring of foreign subsidiaries. The advertising business was developed to promote large sales in a mass market. Railroads merged into a few large systems. Department store chains were created out of previously independent local stores.

The method of studying and evaluating the operation of large enterprises known as *systems analysis* came into being. The computer became an essential instrument in the operation of business offices, banks, school systems, and government agencies. Everything that could be ordered and arranged mechanically was subjected to the computer. Education then came under examination as a candidate for the computer, the teaching machine, and the planned system. Several large corporations were formed for the large scale processing of the teaching and learning operations.

Values are changing with respect to the conduct of business, governmental, and educational processes in ways which are only dimly understood today. Things which can be done efficiently by large organizations and by computers may come to be valued simply because they are more easily obtained or achieved than other things. Forms of learning which can be promoted by computers may come to be favored over other forms of learning. Forms of amusement which can be purveyed through mass media may become the most popular forms of amusement. Ways of working with other people which are most effective in large organizations may become the most highly valued ways of working.

To the criticisms implied by these remarks the proponents of bigness and computerized processes respond that the greater efficiency of these processes will win time and resources for other activities that are valued by people. People can master big organizations and the computer and make them serve a variety of human values. For example, programed teaching may be used to make drills on factual knowledge more efficient so as to gain time for the teacher to work with pupils on other highly valued outcomes of education.

The interaction between values and the complexity of the setting in which people live and work and play is now taking place in ways we do not fully understand, but are trying to use for better living.

C. THE LEISURED SOCIETY

Our society has changed from an economy of scarcity to one of abundance in one generation, after centuries in which we learned to value work as a means of overcoming scarcity. The Protestant ethic was adopted by Western Europe and North America when it appeared that by means of hard work all or a large part of society could lift itself above the poverty level. Work became the axis of life. Education and religion combined to glorify work, and the principal function of education came to be preparation for productive work.

The period of 1900-1920 saw the rise of the United States as an industrial society, with an enormous domestic purchasing power and some export possibilities. Mass production methods were developed and productivity per man-hour began to increase. Wages and salaries increased slowly in purchasing power. Then, as real income reached reasonably satisfactory levels for working people, the work-week was shortened, and first the forty-eight-hour week, then the forty-four-hour, and then the forty-hour week became customary in industry and business.

Throughout this period production was a virtue, and consumption was supposed to be limited to bare needs of people. Anything above this level of consumption was regarded as almost sinful. Veblen's phrase "conspicuous consumption" came to mean a wasteful vice in which a few rich people indulged.

The 1920's and 1930's were a period of confusion in the American economy out of which emerged the conviction that the government could and should intervene in the economic system to prevent deflation and unemployment.

With the great economic boom of the post World War II period, the country soon reached the point where overproduction was a danger, and underconsumption a problem. From this time, the virtues of work began to recede in importance compared with the virtues of consumption.

The widely held view that men should have a right to work as much as they please and as long as they please, provided their work was of good quality, began to be replaced by the view that the work-life and the work-year and the work-week should be limited so as to spread the work among men and women aged twenty to sixty-five, with longer and longer annual vacations. People who insisted on keeping at work after age sixty-five came to be criticized in some quarters as "selfish," "refusing to make way for younger people."

For a decade now, thoughtful people have asked for a reappraisal of the place of work in the hierarchy of personal and social values. They have talked of the values of *consumption* as well as the values of *production*. The *leisured society* is shifting people's attention to the values of leisure, whereby they will consume goods and services in ways which are judged to be personally and socially desirable.

It is clear that life in the future will be less taken up with work, and more with living. But what does it mean to say that we can spend more time in living and less time in working? It means that we will have more free time. Free time in an underdeveloped economy is an unexploited resource for a needed expansion in production. Free time in a modern overproductive economy is itself a product of the economy and calls out to be used wisely, but not for more material production.

What people do with their free time is the major human concern of our society. How they use space is incidental to their use of time. Thus time is the arena in which the drama of human development unfolds in our society. Free time is a promontory of the future jutting into the present—a kind of concrete, present utopia. In Thomas More's *Utopia*, people worked only six hours a day. We have now reached that state.

Free time activities have been placed in three categories:

    service to others;

    contemplation, study, and reflection;

    spontaneous play.

The first two categories involve familiar values which have been recognized and highly regarded for a long time. But the category of play is one we are only beginning to take seriously as a pervasive aspect of living throughout the life cycle. The new ethics of the use of time includes a set of *moral* standards and a set of *aesthetic* standards applied to play.

The most significant resources for the use of free time will all be looked at with much greater attention to their possibilities. Some of these resources are:

1. *The Use of the Outdoors.* As the population increases and the society becomes more urbanized, the outdoors will become increasingly precious as a leisure-time resource, and at the same time the outdoors will be increasingly threatened by the incursions of urbanism and technology. Air and water pollution threaten to make the outdoors unsafe in many areas. Industrial exploitation of the rivers, lakeshore, seashore, and mineral deposits endanger the recreational use of the outdoors.

There is need for a clear statement of the functions of leisure activity and a policy of using the outdoors to serve these functions. Three functions of leisure in a crowded urban society are:

    a. to give isolation, at times, amid the shoving and sprinting and raucous activities of the city;

    b. to reduce nervous tensions through an effective combination of physical and mental activity;

    c. to provide a setting for the experience of awe and reverence for things that are not man-made.

2. *Television.* Mr. Lee Loevinger, a member of the Federal Communications Commission, told the twentieth annual convention of the New Jersey Broadcasters Association, "It seems to me that television is the literature of the illiterate, the culture of the lowborn, the wealth of the poor, the privilege of the underprivileged, the exclusive club of the excluded masses. . . . Television is a golden goose that lays scrambled eggs. And it is futile and probably fatal to beat it for not laying caviar. Anyway, more people like scrambled eggs than caviar."[1]

This view of TV as an element in the mass culture will be challenged as the federal government moves to establish "public television" which will be separate from the advertising business. The Carnegie Corporation comments, "What commercial television cannot do because of its need to reach mass audiences, noncommercial television cannot do because it lacks the money, facilities, and personnel. Hence in the technologically most advanced society in the history of man, the greatest technological device for informing, delighting, inspiring, amusing, provoking, and entertaining remains pitiably unexploited, and the American public is the loser."[2]

With the Ford Foundation also interested in making non-commercial television a force for better use of free time, it is clear that there will be a public television network financed at a level of at least $100 million a year. This network will assist the 124 existing educational television stations and will provide programs that go beyond the bounds of what is ordinarily called educational television.

3. *The Performing Arts.* It is generally claimed that there has been a kind of "cultural explosion" in the United States since World War II. The number of symphony orchestras doubled in twenty years, to a total of more than 1400. The number of groups presenting opera doubled to 754 in the decade before 1964.[3] Much of this growth was in the amateur sector. Of 1401 symphony orchestras only 54 were composed predominantly of professional musicians. Two economists looked at the phenomenon with a critical eye and concluded that much of the increase between 1946 and 1963 was due to growth in population and increase in prices, as well as increase in real income, rather than an increase in interest in the arts compared with interest in other activities.[4] It was concluded that substantial subsidy from the federal government is needed to give the performing arts the kind of development they deserve.

4. *National Foundation for the Arts and Humanities.* The bill that was signed into law on September 29, 1965, may go down in history as the most important piece of legislation for that year, and perhaps for that decade. Thus the national government acknowledged responsibility for the state of the arts and for the functioning of the arts in the improvement of the mass culture. Before that time, a number of states had set up state councils on the arts with programs that included: sponsoring touring groups in the performing arts, art exhibitions, conferences on music, and providing technical assistance to local community groups that supported museums, galleries, theater, and music groups. While the amounts of money provided for the state councils have been modest, and the budget of the Foundation for the Arts and Humanities was only $12 million in its second year, the money has already set in motion some promising programs.

The level of federal government support for the performing arts will certainly advance to at least $100 million annually within the next decade, and this will support work in major regional centers in addition to assisting the state councils in their programs.

## II. Values and the Social Setting

Having surveyed the three areas of social change and social problems that are producing the major value changes in our society, we now turn to the actual value changes. We can discern some values which are receding in social importance, some that continue into the new social setting with little or no change, and some that emerge in the new social setting.

### A. RECEDING VALUES

Values which are receding in prevalence, especially among young people, are the following:

| PERSONAL | SOCIAL |
|---|---|
| individual saving and thrift | nationalistic, provincial, and |
| work as a major source of self-respect | parochial preferences |

There has been a recession in the extent to which people favor their own country, state, region, race, and religion on the basis of simple prejudice and absolutistic, black-white judgments. This is a part of the *open society* ideology. It is recognized that people of other social groups than one's own are generally as good and as bad as one's own group. It is also recognized that most people tend to favor their own social group; this prejudice is regarded as desirable, but also as a prejudice.

The value of individual saving has decreased in importance, probably for two reasons. First, material goods have become so cheap and so easily replaceable that there is very little practical value in saving old clothes, paper, rubber, bottles, and junk of various kinds. Consequently, people place less value on saving and using material goods over and over again. The saving of money is different, since money is always useful. But there is greater value placed on spending money for goods and services needed now and less on saving money for future uses. One's future economic security depends upon government social security, government services, and forced automatic saving through social security taxation to a much greater extent than it did formerly, when a person was taught that he must save, personally, "for a rainy day."

The value of working steadily and productively as a basis for one's self-respect has receded for some young people—probably only among a minority of them. For those who are not able to get steady employment this fact must either undermine their self-respect, or they must separate self-respect from work. Both things have happened. A considerable fraction, both urban and rural, has deflated the value of work and based their sense of self-respect upon other characteristics.

B. STABLE VALUES

A great mass of values has continued pretty much unchanged throughout this century, though their relative importance has shifted in many cases, and their conventional forms of expression have often changed.

These values may be categorized as *personal* and *social* according to the following scheme:

| PERSONAL | SOCIAL |
|---|---|
| autonomy | loyalty to one's society |
| rational conscience | friendliness |
| rational foresight | social responsibility |
| instrumental activism | family interaction |
| achievement motivation | social progress and social |
| productivity | change |
| worship | |

The list of *personal* values is a standard list of the virtues we have come to associate with middle-class American life. Though some profess to believe that these values are losing some of their high standing in contemporary American life, this writer can see no convincing evidence of this. The combination of autonomy with rational foresight and internalized moral control may seem to some researchers to be at variance with the other-directedness that David Reisman describes as increasingly characteristic of contemporary man in America, but there is no empirical evidence known to the writer which points to a decrease of autonomy and rational foresight either in fact or in value. There does seem to be some increase in cooperativeness in group behavior which might be called other-directedness, but this does not appear to reduce the value of autonomy.

The instrumental activism combined with a high value on productivity and achievement motivation which Talcott Parsons sees as characteristic of valued behavior in the American middle class is as much desired now as it was ten or twenty years ago. Only the goals of productivity and of achievement may be changing from material goods to other less tangible forms of goods.

Loyalty to one's societal group (nation, race, religion, etc.) appears to be a major value that is not receding, though people are becoming less chauvinistic and more rational and relativistic in their loyalties. Friendliness and a sense of responsibility for the welfare of others are values of long standing. The value of interaction and mutual assistance within the three-generation and the extended family appears to be as great both in practice and in verbal allegiance as it was in an earlier day, despite some sociological theorizing about the narrowing values of the nuclear family. Social progress and social change have generally been expected and valued in America throughout the present century.

C. EMERGING VALUES

Values which seem to be emerging in the contemporary social setting are the following:

| PERSONAL | SOCIAL |
|---|---|
| expressive activity | international and ecumenical cooperation |
| aesthetic appreciation | |
| widening and deepening of experience | intranational opportunity and justice |
| tolerance of complexity and ambiguity | agape—service in an open society |
| | organizational loyalty and cooperation |

Expressive activity is distinguished from instrumental activity by the fact that expressive activity has the activity itself as a goal, while instrumental activity is a means to an end outside of the activity. Thus, a person who studies a foreign language "for fun" is engaging in an expressive activity, while one who studies the foreign language in order to qualify for a certain job is engaging in instrumental activity. The great increase in free time gives opportunity for more expressive activities and tends to increase the value of this kind of activity.

Along with increased value on expressive activity goes greater value on aesthetic appreciation—that is, on exploring the aesthetic qualities of the things and activities which come into one's experience.

The greater value placed on the widening and deepening of experience is a phenomenon which is undoubtedly present, but about which we are ambivalent. There seems to be a cult of "experience for the sake of experience" developing. An example which disturbs many people is the smoking of marijuana and the taking of LSD by some young people who say they do this kind of thing "for kicks."

The notion of experience for the sake of experience, without placing differential values on different forms of experience, is profoundly disturbing to those who see in this phenomenon a sure sign of decadence. This writer shares this view. A long-term policy of gaining experience just for the sake of experience, without applying standards of value to experience, seems to deny the existence of some kinds of experience that are better than other kinds. But a temporary period of wide experimentation with a variety of expressive activities may be a means of discovering new values in free-time activity and may be justified as a kind of exploration into *terra incognita* that may lead to important aesthetic discoveries.

With the opening up of the world of free time, combined with the growing complexity of the world of work, it seems likely that the ability to tolerate and even to enjoy complexity and ambiguity will become more highly valued. This ability is highly valued for executives and decision-makers in the world of production today. A person with this ability can stand to live and work in a situation which is open-ended, has many possibilities, and where solutions of problems must be worked out flexibly. Since the coming of more free time introduces even more complexity into the life of the average person, this quality is likely to be valued more highly.

Emerging social values are a response to the movement toward an *open society* within the nation and among the nations. Greater value will be set on the social and political measures that make for cooperation, opportunity, and justice between and within social, racial, and national groups. The movement among the great religions for ecumenical cooperation may give greater impetus to this value than the parallel movement among the nations of the world.

The principal social value emerging out of the *open society* is the form of love we know as *agape*, or charity. This is the value that gives such dynamic force to the Peace Corps, VISTA, and other volunteer activities.

Finally, the value placed on loyalty and cooperation within an organization is increasing. This is a necessary concomitant of the growth in size and complexity of organizations in the economic, governmental, and educational spheres.

## III. Young People and Their Values

Young people are especially sensitive to the social trends that produce value changes. It appears that they respond most readily to the trends toward an *open society* and toward a *leisured society,* and some of them appear to resist the trend toward a *technocratic society.*

There are adult voices speaking against the values fostered by the *technocratic society,* and they appear to represent some young people. Paul Goodman calls ours the *empty society* and comments that our satisfaction diminishes as our standard of living increases. In his Massey Lectures, *The Moral Ambiguity of America,*[5] he contends that our society has few alternatives to a regimented life for average people. For instance, young people are forced to go to school whether they like it or not, because there is no acceptable alternative. He thinks young people would like more freedom in a more open world.

The truth is, of course, that young people are a highly variegated lot, with a variegated set of values. Accepting the proposition that young people should be seen as members of a variety of subgroups with respect to their values, we have recognized eight categories or varieties of youth (see figure). Each of the subgroups has its own predominant values.

1 and 2. *Radical Activists and Concerned Liberals.* These two groups are characterized by emerging values, especially the social values of: service in an open society; intranational opportunity and justice; and international and ecumenical cooperation. They also have strongly developed most of the stable values, and especially those of social progress and social change, social responsibility, and instrumental activism.

3. *Hippies and Yippies.* This group, seen as perplexing and disturbing by the adult generation, prizes the emerging values. The widening and deepening of experience are major values for them and lead them into forms of experimentation with themselves that are profoundly alarming to adults. They set a high value on expressive activity, and on some forms of aesthetic appreciation. Their slogan of love is probably best interpreted as a combination of *philos* (brotherly love) and *agape* (charity). As long as this group exists separate from and unabsorbable by the mainstream of American culture, it must stand as a matter of deep concern for adults who are aware of social change and its influence on the values of society. Our society has not made full use of its potential for improvement of life if it forces the exponents of its emerging values to live on the margins of society.

## VARIETIES OF YOUTH

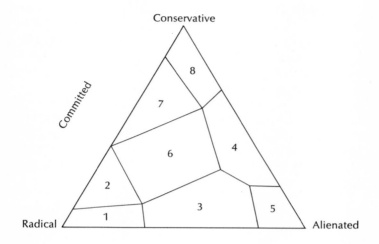

| Per Cent | Category |
|---|---|
| 5 | 1. Radical Activists (New Left) |
| 15 | 2. Concerned Liberals |
| 10 | 3. Hippies and Yippies |
| 10 | 4. Uncommitted |
| 5 | 5. Amoral Hostiles |
| 35 | 6. Common Man Complacents—Squares |
| 15 | 7. Concerned Conservatives |
| 5 | 8. Reactionary Activists |

4. *The Uncommitted.* This group as described by Keniston in his book, *The Uncommitted,*[6] is alienated from, but not actively hostile to, the society around them. They lack both the self-assurance and the social fidelity that would lead them toward action on behalf of social change. They are low on the stable values of social loyalty and social responsibility. Their principal motivating

values are for a widening and deepening of experience and for aesthetic appreciation.

5. *Amoral Hostiles.* This alienated group does not share in the broad social values of the society but has socially narrow values, such as intense peer group loyalty, autonomy, and a desire for expressive activities that are exciting and dangerous.

6. *Common Man Complacents.* The large group of common man complacents of course maintain the stable values, with special strength in productivity, achievement motivation, social responsibility, friendliness, and family interaction.

7 and 8. *Reactionary Activists and Concerned Conservatives.* These two groups are the opposite of the preceding group, and they tend toward the receding values of nationalistic and provincial preferences, individual saving, and thrift. They also maintain the stable values of loyalty to one's society, autonomy, and productivity.

## IV. Conclusion

As we study the changing value structure of our society by observing the ways in which the younger generation relates itself to the tasks of growing up and achieving identity, we come to two significant conclusions: first, social change is promoting value changes at a pace and in a direction that is disturbing to many of the older generation; and second, the educational system has a major responsibility for developing forms of education which help young people to become effective carriers of the new values in a democratic, highly productive society with growing amounts of free time for its members.

## REFERENCES

1. Lee Loevinger, 20th Annual Convention of the New Jersey Broadcasters Association.
2. Carnegie *Quarterly*, Vol. 15, No. 1, Winter 1967.

3. *The Performing Arts: Problems and Prospects; Report on the Future of Theatre, Dance, Music in America*, New York: McGraw-Hill, 1965, pp. 21, 28.

4. W. J. Baumol and W. G. Bowen, *Performing Arts: The Economic Dilemma*, New York: The Twentieth Century Fund, 1966.

5. Paul Goodman, *The Moral Ambiguity of America*. (Massey Lectures)

6. Kenneth Keniston, *The Uncommitted: Alienated Youth in American Society*, New York: Harcourt, Brace & World, 1965.

# Attitudes and Values of College Students

DANA L. FARNSWORTH, M.D.

In many ways a college's relationship with students is parental—in the fullest, most positive sense of that word. The institution must teach, support, inspire, guide, discipline; the student's simultaneous tasks are inheriting and outgrowing.

Impatience is natural, but students who are controlled by it need help. People of college age tend to be more adventurous, intense, radical, impulsive, and idealistic than the adults who are their "caretakers." Students have difficulty in defining the relationship between freedom and authority, between authority and authoritarianism. They are idealistic, and to some of them anything less than all-out action represents a compromise.

It is clear that there are very few simple or comprehensive answers, but those who are in a position to influence college students can help them focus on what is relevant, and can help them marshal their interests and energies constructively rather than practice self-damaging and useless gestures against authority.

There are currently more than seven million students enrolled in American colleges and universities. The size of this number, and the fact that the human beings involved attend institutions which themselves differ greatly, make it impossible to consider college students as a homogeneous group. There are as many differences among these young people as among members of the population at large. But they do have in common their age, academic status, and developmental stage, which provide a basis for considering them *en masse*. An all-inclusive "in general" should be understood to underlie the following discussion, not only because of individual variations and exceptions but because it reflects one person's experience and interpretation. The discussion is not intended as an analysis of the causes *per se* of

22

riots, but rather as an examination of some of the fundamental causes behind students' discontent with their college experience.

This increasing discontent, as expressed in increasingly vigorous forms of dissent, has caught most educators and investigators with their explanatory hypotheses unformed and inadequate.[1] However, scientific studies which supplement clinical observations of college students' attitudes and values are increasing in number and scope.[2] The extensive studies conducted by the Harvard University Health Services, whose collective title is *The Harvard Student Study,* are nearing completion after ten years of data collection and analysis. My own observations and conclusions are in accord with reports from that project but have been made quite independently.

In many ways a college's relationship with students is parental —in the fullest, most positive sense of that word. The institution's functions include teaching, supporting, inspiring, guiding, disciplining; the student's simultaneous tasks are inheriting and outgrowing. Confronted with tradition, he must decide how much is usable and relevant, how much must eventually be discarded—and this decision must not be made mindlessly but in a context of information.

This is a complex task, because the student's growth is not merely academic, it is emotional and social as well. Ideally, these components are in balance, but in actuality such harmony is rare, particularly in adolescence. The student must extend his old skills and learn new ones. He must learn new roles. If he is fortunate, his previous experiences have been a preparation, and he avoids a disturbing sense of shock or discontinuity. (However, even the best-prepared student undergoes some dislocation or shaking up in making the transition to college, although instead of being immediately apparent it may take the form of a delayed reaction, such as the infamous "sophomore slump.") Moreover, he must learn to integrate his new roles or to come to terms with the conflicts inherent in them, to reconcile emotional, professional, familial, and societal demands, and to work out meaningful and constructive priorities. Confronted with such problems, a young person's temptation is to short-circuit the process, either by denying that the problems exist or by acknowledging them but acting prematurely.

College students have in common with other young people many maturational tasks and "universal" experiences. However, the particulars differ and the setting is unique. The college atmosphere is a relatively homogeneous and sheltered one; its population is, by nature, transient. A student is allotted four years to obtain a bachelor's degree, whether this period of time is appropriate to his needs or not. (Current draft laws virtually preclude male students' taking leaves of absence unless the student is in dire psychological straits.) For many students, college is a time of uncertainty or even anxiety, with current pressures and the threat (for the fortunate ones, a promise) of adult responsibility; at the same time there persists the romantic myth of the "golden years," unaccompanied by stress or obligation. But college is also an exciting, productive period, one which makes available myriad new intellectual and social pleasures. These too are part of the student's "task."

The student-college relationship is reciprocal. Just as parents and children interact to become a unit that is more than the sum of its parts, i.e., a family, so do students, faculty, and administration act and respond and learn with each other. The student's inheritance is knowledge and, by extension, judgment—which may ultimately reject part of what created and nourished it. But it is not education's purpose to perpetuate itself unchanged; rather, its aim is one of evolution and continuous relevance. The processes of inheriting and outgrowing are gradual, concomitant, and cyclical, and take place as individuals respond to new information of all kinds. It is a parental function, a function of guidance, to make use of those constructive elements that already exist or are potential, to focus on a student's areas of strength and help develop them further, and to acquaint young people with all the choices. Having done this in good faith, the "parent's" underlying attitude must be one of confidence in the student's ability to carry on effectively.

If education were merely a matter of accumulating facts, academic institutions would have to be no more than libraries and facilities for data retrieval. Happily, there is no college which operates on this assumption. In general, education is seen not as a fixed, inviolable package of information but as a process in which the actual facts communicated (which themselves are subject to change and re-interpretation) are less important than their context, the attitudes, values, and assumptions underlying them. Furthermore, academic accomplishment does not occur in a vacuum. Intellectual excitement is communicable, the pleasures of both rigorous thought and disciplined creativity are learned largely through precept and example, and interest and passion are best learned from teachers who are themselves personally and passionately involved, both in their own disciplines and in the whole educational process. The techniques of the medieval craft guilds and the relationship of artists to their protégés, with their "laying on of hands," are pertinent to college education.

The fundamental educational assumption is, of course, that intellectual concerns and activities have value, and that their value is twofold: they are exciting and deeply pleasurable (in a serious sense) in themselves, and they are connected with man's best aspirations for his own life and human life in general. Intellectual effort of a high order is unique in man and characteristic of him. Man can survive many deprivations, but absence of thought is not one of them if he is still to be described as "human."

A second educational assumption, which is an extension of the first, is that the disciplines of college are not ends in themselves but tools for learning concepts, approaches, methods, and data made meaningful by informed interpretation: what do facts mean, what are their uses? Educators hope to stimulate independent and creative thought; this is the essence of "higher learning." Charles Frankel, professor of philosophy at Columbia and formerly Assistant Secretary of State, has defined an intellectual as one who can deal with the world with and through symbols, one who can think hypothetically, one who can think about that which does not exist, and who can look upon his own society with detachment.[3]

Such intellectual activity may lead to dissent, but it is often dissent of a creative kind, and not merely criticism of the old ways. In fact, the great intellectual revolutions are, by their very nature, dissensions (Freud and Einstein, for example), but their focus is on the constructive and positive—the creative. Indeed, this kind of achievement depends much less on the ability to perceive the inadequacies or defects in traditional approaches than on the ability to invent new approaches, to hypothesize, to work out possibilities for which there has been little or no previous evidence. The Danish scientist, mathematician, inventor, and poet Piet Hein has said:

> . . . the creative process is the same in all fields. You can say about art—meaning the inner psychological side of the creative process—that it is the process of solving problems that cannot be stated clearly before they are solved. The process of orientation to a new problem is practically one hundred per cent of the solution. Once you've formulated the problem its just table work.[4]

While not all college students are sufficiently creative or intelligent (or sincerely motivated) to be artists or intellectual revolutionaries, these basic attitudes and values are still pertinent to their educations. Rote learning is (at best) useless; the sense of the worth of intellectual activities and of the methods of reason, logic, and analysis remains long after specific facts are forgotten and provides a context and approach for all future material.

By the time a person reaches college his personality patterns have been fairly well established, although they are not immutable. In addition to his individual biological and psychological "givens" he has had many experiences within his family and his various social groups, all of which determine in part who he is and how he responds to college. Young people are unusually vulnerable to stress if their histories include: parental discord; lack of love and parental approval; lack of firm, friendly, and consistent discipline; marked conflict between the values of home and school. Feelings of isolation, hostility, and worthlessness predispose students to break down or decompensate.

Instances in which material and cultural deprivation work in anyone's favor are rare; sometimes such disadvantages work as a spur to motivation, but often they exact a steep price, such as "culture shock." The latter, however, is not limited to interaction between higher and lower socioeconomic groups; a youngster from an isolated or rural background, for instance, may undergo profound upheaval at an urban college.

Since human beings are whole entities, and all their concerns and behavior are components and manifestations of a single personality, it is somewhat arbitrary to talk about the separate issues with which students must come to terms. Some divisions are necessary, of course, if there is to be any discussion, but it must be remembered that the categories overlap and interlock and also exist on many levels (personal, social, psychological, ethical) sumultaneously. Every human "solution" depends on the individual's sense of his identity.

The most comprehensive and useful conceptualization of personality growth has been Erikson's formulation of eight stages of psychosocial development in the human life cycle, each characterized by a special "task" and "crisis" which must be worked through if the next stage is to be reached. A full presentation of this material appears in *Childhood and Society*[5]; while all the stages are interrelated, the two with which college students are actively involved are adolescence and young adulthood.

In early adolescence the rapid body growth and the accompanying sexual maturation force the young person to reconsider his prior assumptions about himself and to "refight many of the earlier battles" which he had considered settled. During this period of uncertainty (identity diffusion), he runs the risk of not being able to organize himself sufficiently in order to use his energies effectively. Or, if loyalties to his parents or friends are not developed or are severely ambivalent, he may consciously or unconsciously attempt to become what they do not want him to be (negative identity). Only when he develops a feeling of security in his own identity is he able to contemplate his own inner feelings and to establish intimacy with others. If he cannot enter into intimate relationships (including, but not limited to, the sexual) with others, because of fear of losing his identity, he may develop a deep sense of isolation. Erikson has said about his work:

> There has been a tendency here and there to turn the eight stages into a sort of rosary of achievement, a device for counting the fruits of each stage—trust, autonomy, initiative, and so forth—as though each were achieved as a permanent trait. People of this bent are apt to leave out the negative counterparts of each stage, as if the healthy personality had permanently conquered these hazards. The fact is that the healthy personality must reconquer them continuously in the same way that the body's metabolism resists decay. All that we learn are certain fundamental means and mechanisms for retaining and regaining mastery. Life is a sequence not only of developmental but also of accidental crises. It is hardest to take when both types of crisis coincide. In each crisis, under favorable conditions, the positive is likely to outbalance the negative, and each reintegration builds strength for the next crisis. But the negative is always with us to some degree in the form of a measure of infantile anxiety, fear of abandonment—a residue of immaturity carried throughout life, which is perhaps the price man has to pay for a childhood long enough to permit him to be the learning and the teaching animal, and thus to achieve his particular mastery of reality. . . . It is the nature of human life that each succeeding crisis takes place within a widened social radius where an ever-larger number of significant persons have a bearing on the outcome. There is in childhood, first, the maternal person, then the parental combination, then the basic family and other instructing adults. Youth demands "confirmation" from strangers who hold to a design of life; and later, the adult needs challenges from mates and partners, and even from his growing children and expanding works, in order to continue to grow himself. And all these relationships must be imbedded in an "ethos," a cultural order, to guide the individual's course. . . . Each further stage of growth in a given individual is not only dependent upon the relatively successful completion of his own previous stages, but also on the completion of the subsequent stages in those

other individuals with whom he interacts and whom he accepts as models.[6]

The significance of these remarks for all educators is obvious.

Most people today would agree that the task of greatest
importance for any person (beyond physical subsistence) is to
determine who he is, and then to make choices consistent with
that knowledge—to discover his own nature and not to violate
it. This process begins very early in life; in fact, it starts with the
child's ability to differentiate between himself and his sur-
roundings. At that point he begins to say *no,* to deal with self-
definition. After he learns to indicate *That person is not me* or
*That procedure is not what I want* he also learns to define
himself positively: *I am the person who* and *I want. . . .*

The cycles of development, recognition, and response never
really end; ideally, an individual continues throughout his life
to be in touch with his talents, knowledge, and patterns of
behavior. Freedom is his ability to be what he wants to be and
do what he wants to do. Of course there can be many restric-
tions, not the least of which are self-imposed.

Freedom is both subjective and relative; merely making a
choice is not synonymous with acting in one's best interest or
enjoying liberty. The Harvard student who said, "Every time
I make a choice I note doors silently closing all around me" is a
dramatic (and pathetic) illustration of the fact that if choice
is arbitrary, irrelevant, premature, or compelled (either psychologically or socially) it represents the opposite of freedom.
Similarly, necessity is not always antagonistic to freedom. For
example, if what one *can* do and what one *wants* to do coincide,
there is not much choice—but for the individual involved there
is no feeling of constraint, either. On the other hand, counselors
often see students who can do several things well and who,
theoretically, should be diversely productive but instead feel
torn apart or inadequate.

In reading himself correctly (no easy achievement) and
acting accordingly insofar as circumstances permit, a person
acknowledges his responsibility to himself. But while the funda-

mental goal for each person is to be himself, it is also true that the world is full of other human beings—and rules, safeguards, schedules, etc. The key word is *other*, with its connotations of foreign, alien, conflicting, hostile—reflecting a human tendency to define everything else as strange, even menacing. (Many primitive tribes call themselves by whatever word in their language means "the people.") In this sense Sartre was right when he wrote, "Hell is other people"; their very existence imposes limitations, if not outright pain. As with individual growth, socialization takes a long time. The acceptance of social responsibility is never a closed issue because it always involves some conflict with personal freedom; to a young person it is the most vital issue. Giving up the dependency and confinement (but also the safety and security) of childhood, he is both impatient and anxious about coming into his own.

The primary struggle occurs with his parents, but it often extends to all authority. It may take a while for students to recognize the distinctions between *authority* and *authoritarianism* and to learn to refrain from automatically and prejudicially equating the two. Students are hardly to be blamed for their confusion in this area, however, since it pervades adult behavior. Hatred of the Chief Executive by those who disagree with him has been customary from Washington's administration to Nixon's. Politicians often encourage the spread of derogatory opinions about their opponents. Parents whose sons or daughters have encountered disciplinary measures by the college or police often blame "the authorities" for creating a society of law in which a particular act becomes a legal infraction.

Students have difficulty defining the relationship between freedom and authority because it is a highly charged issue for them and because their stage of development renders them especially sympathetic to underdogs, to the politically and socially dispossessed. Being idealistic and energetic, they find the conservative attitudes of some of their elders unacceptable and the failure to combat injustice cowardly and dishonest. However, such concern is not merely a psychological "fixation" limited to adolescence or an emotional phase to be outgrown or resolved. The subject of resistance to authority is part of the ongoing human dialogue: the legal and moral considerations; differences between unlawful behavior arising from a sense of moral outrage and that with antisocial motivations; modes and limits; the conflict between the ideal and the actual; the extent to which compliance and failure to protest constitute collaboration in immoral acts. Those who see history as more than a series of dates have learned—World War II and the Nazi crimes against humanity were instrumental in bringing the lesson home—the significance of sins of omission, and today many people believe that if they do not bear witness and take action against injustice, oppression, and war they are as guilty as those who perpetuate these evils.

Since college students are actively engaged in becoming adults, no administration can take an attitude of "Because I say so" without being inconsistent and hypocritical. Colleges must maintain their organization without authoritarianism, not merely because students will no longer tolerate it but because it precludes possibilities for creativity and involvement and thus negates the aims of education. Moreover, students learn a great deal from explanations of why, if rules or procedures cannot be changed, they must remain as they are; acquainting young people with the facts and the bases for decisions helps them to develop into the informed responsible people which institutions of higher learning hope for; it also increases their sense of identification with and responsibility toward those institutions. And it is not unlikely that students may make valuable contributions, provided that they are not regarded as children who should be seen and not heard.

As students come to recognize these value problems, as well as the differences between generational values and modes, they have resorted more and more to violence. Riots, student strikes, "sit-ins," "mill-ins," "liberation" of college buildings, and impeding freedom of passage to college officials and representatives of the military services and commercial firms have become commonplace. This crescendo of violence has stimulated a wide variety of explanations of its origin. As students see a society phenomenally successful in producing material goods but notably unsuccessful in assuring equitable distribution, they begin to ask questions regarding other societal shortcomings. What about civil rights for everyone? Who speaks for the poor? Why is war necessary to solve problems between nations? Not realizing that these are very complex, perhaps insoluble, issues whose resolution involves fundamental changes in the attitudes of many people (including some who will suffer in the process), they look for scapegoats. Government representatives and administrators of colleges and universities fulfill this role admirably, not because they are not trying but because they are not succeeding, and above all, because they are there.

One of the paradoxes in student dissatisfaction is the apparent lack of correlation between the attempts institutions have made to meet students' needs and the students' response to such efforts. For example, student criticisms of the administrative structure and social organization at Columbia in 1968 were quite similar to those made by Harvard students in 1969, even though the two Harvard members of the Cox Commission saw great differences between the two institutions in their attitudes toward students. The tactics practiced by student protest organizers were practically the same at both colleges, the quality of language was nearly identical, as was the use of "inflated rhetoric" to sway opinion. In both instances, a small hard-core group of extremists was able, by forcing police action, to politicize or radicalize large segments of the previously moderate or liberal students.

Young people come by their activism honestly by virtue of their age and national tradition. American history reflects a belief in men's rights to bring about political and social change, starting with the Pilgrims and continuing to the Western frontier, where the concept of individual rights and freedom was extended to the point of taking the law into one's own hands. At its best this country represents freedom of expression—in fact, the democratic process depends on this. It also depends on the maintenance of a line between constructive, lawful activism and anarchy. The boundary cannot, of course, be fixed

—it shifts with particular conditions and situations. But the transition into areas of destructive activity occurs when protest becomes self-perpetuating and the style is carried on for its own sake. (When asked, "What are you all against?" the leader of a motorcycle gang replied, "What do you have?—and we're against it.")

Certain social, political, and psychological facts of American life are inescapable. The frontier and the town meeting, with their opportunities for geographical escape and individual effectiveness, are almost gone. Complex technology, IBM-card bureaucracy, and a sense of personal impotence prevail; the man-made is an anachronism or a luxury. Traditional assumptions, myths, and possibilities are breaking down, and many of the old American dreams are being satirized, scientifically disproved, or rendered morally unacceptable. Above all looms the threat of nuclear disaster, of total annihilation triggered by accident or unpredictable and unpreventable events.

In the last few years the rate of social change has increased beyond anything occurring in the past. Communication is becoming all-pervasive; but the present communication networks distort their message by the tendency to overemphasize the violent, the abnormal, the grotesque aspects of human behavior and to neglect the myriad phenomena that add meaning, quality, and dignity to life. Our governments have devised far more effective means of destroying human life and property than of safeguarding it. Negative forces of greed, hostility, and intolerance constantly limit those forces seeking to improve social and economic status, establish higher health standards, and develop meaningful training of youth.

Many of our people, young and old, are angry, confused, dismayed, and justifiably alarmed. They see the deprivations to which others are subjected, and the failure of projects designed to minimize poverty and racial injustice. They see the inability of their government to solve the problem of the Vietnam war. They see urban decay, rural dilapidation, air and water pollution, the population avalanche, exploitation, and violence. Above all, they see the discrepancy between the American

Dream and what they see in private and public life. They are in revolt, not against the older generation's values, but because the older generation does not practice those values to which it gives lip service.

It is no wonder that many people, students among them, feel powerless, and that there is a widespread sense, particularly on the part of the young, of being in the grip of impersonal forces, resistance to which must be of extreme form or intensity to have any effect. But the belief that they must take drastic steps to make an impression causes many young people to over-react as a matter of policy, and in fact sometimes to carry protest to the point of self-destruction. (Suicidal behavior more commonly accompanies personal and family conflicts, and in such cases is literal and immediate, but anyone whose life style is limited to protest is also killing himself.)

This tendency toward extremism and protest is in part a product of affluence, simply because young people have the time and energy for it. They are not constantly involved in making a living or coping with external dangers. But this in no way means that the students' concerns are unimportant or invalid; on the contrary, they must be considered seriously and with respect. They are real, disturbing, and sometimes overwhelming, and while one may wish that students dealt with them differently, one cannot dismiss them as meaningless. In fact, helping students find constructive modes of action is one of the jobs of college faculty members and administrators— but to do so they must believe that the students' concerns are significant. It is clear that there are very few simple or comprehensive answers, but those who are in a position to influence college students can help them focus on what is relevant and can help them marshal their interests and energies constructively rather than practice the self-damaging and useless gestures of cheating, vandalism, and violence.

Young people often fail to realize the fact that inappropriate, shocking, or offensive protest focuses the opposition's attention on the style, not the content, so that there occurs a fusion of the two which defeats the basic purpose. Such protest elicits an answer to the wrong question, but one it has inadvertently raised itself. The two simultaneous issues provoke (and allow) simplistic responses to complex questions. Most people do not stop to understand that the style may be irrelevant to a valid message, and they become fixed on the former and respond only to it. This does not mean that protestors should never attract attention (that also would be self-defeating), but that they must learn how to be effective and not detract from the real point, and how to avoid violating others' rights while doing so.

How much tradition to use and when to "break out" are also issues for conformists, but these people are less disruptive and therefore more convenient to society. Their solutions may be equally self-limiting, but since they don't disrupt the status quo they do not provoke negative reactions.

> Some delinquents, perhaps in their determination to be themselves at all costs and under terrible conditions, have more strength and a greater potential for contributing to the richness of the national life than do many excessively conforming or neurotically defeatist members of their generation, who have given up youth's prerogatives to dream and to dare. We must study this problem until we can overcome the kind of outraged bewilderment which makes the adult world seem untrustworthy to youth and hence may seem to justify the choice of a delinquent identity.
>
> Actually, transitory delinquency, as well as other forms of antisocial or asocial behavior, often may be what I have called a psychosocial moratorium—a period of delay in the assumption of adult commitment. Some youths need a period of relaxed expectations, of guidance to the various possibilities for positive identification through opportunities to participate in adult work, or even of introspection and experimentation—none of which can be replaced by either moralistic punishment or condescending forgiveness.[7]

Students are well aware of how things should be, but they know less about practical techniques. (Of course, practicality or easiness is not the only criterion for action; if it were, social progress would be minimal, and it is fortunate for all of us that some of us aim high.) Rand Rosenblatt (Harvard '66) wrote in the Harvard *Crimson* 1966 Commencement Supplement that the student radical "is caught in the tension between the vision of a high potential and the inertia of the actual, and does not know exactly what to do."[8]

The disparities between goals and pratices are expressed in the phrase "politics is the art of the possible." The idealistic would consider this limitation by (and concession to) the possible a perversion and defeat of human aspirations. And sometimes it is, but not always. Ideals cannot be achieved by fiat; human effort, sometimes expended for a long time without dramatic results, is required. Writing also in the Commencement Supplement, Michael D. Barone (Harvard '66) expressed his belief "that this generation of Harvard students is going to remain more committed—in a quiet and unobtrusive way—than its predecessors to improving our society through personal effort and government action."[9]

Feelings of powerlessness are at least humiliating and at worst may be completely defeating. But activism and protest demonstrations are not the only ways of dealing with a sense of impotence. Most children learn ways of "getting around" their parents without precipitating open conflict or armed aggression; often these maneuvers are mutually recognized (without being explicitly acknowledged) and serve as safety valves or escape routes. But sometimes they extend and rigidify into a style in which results justify techniques for achieving them, manipulation is the *modus operandi*, and the person who refuses to employ the short-cuts and gambits may suffer materially.

College students are often quite adept at such gamesmanship; one Harvard undergraduate reported a conversation in which an informal group spent half an hour discussing a book which not one of the members had read. Although such a situation is rare (it is to be hoped) in classrooms, it exemplifies a mode. The temptation to get by on such ploys is immense, because of students' past success with such behavior, academic pressures, and the appeal of "sophistication." But students who have some glimpse of the real meaning of education find that succeeding without trying is not sufficiently gratifying. It reduces academic pursuits to games or contests; furthermore, it depends on the attention and admiration of others for its real success. (Many students who seem to study very little actually work very hard, but secretly, because the "fun" is in giving the impression of doing nothing.) This attitude is often relinquished when students become interested enough in their studies, and particularly when they undertake independent and creative projects rather than doing work which mainly involves rote learning.

The real problem occurs when manipulation and sidestepping become a person's characteristic way of dealing with everything. Such individuals habitually fail to confront the major issues and tasks, repeatedly avoid working out situations which must be dealt with if any maturation is to take place, and never develop adequate emotional and intellectual techniques and satisfactions. Most young people have a tendency, as Robert Frost said in another context, "to try to get ahead before they have caught up," but a tendency is not a life style. Impatience is natural, but students who are controlled by it need help.

Psychiatrists at the Harvard University Health Services report a noticeable decrease, over the past few years, in students' abilities to control impulsive behavior—and the trend is not limited to Harvard students. Both individual (psychological) and social factors contribute to this situation.

As I have noted above, impulsivity is characteristic of this age group, and learning "disciplined and devoted delay" (with regard to all categories, not just sexuality) is its major developmental task. However, in order to be willing to subordinate immediate pleasures, a person must have a firm faith in the eventual rewards. The amount of frustration which individuals can tolerate varies, but in general the practice of self-control seems useless or even foolish without subsequent gain. A student's previous experiences greatly influence his capacities for productive waiting. If his past lessons have indicated that self-control is synonymous with deprivation, it is unlikely that he will refrain from trying to get what he wants right away, regardless of the consequences to himself and others. In fact, he is unlikely to be much concerned with others at all—he expends all his energies in "looking out for Number One."

The ability and willingness to postpone the payoff is as pertinent to individual efforts as it is to social activities—in fact, it is one of the basic elements in creativity. A work of art may not necessarily take a long time to produce, but often enough the process takes longer than the artist would like and reward is often delayed. However, this lack is of a social or external reward; the personal satisfaction from the process itself is sufficient to keep the artist at his self-appointed task. Such creativity for its own sake illustrates the importance to his endeavors of a person's *commitment*. This term enjoys such wide currency that it is often reduced to cant or meaninglessness, but in actuality it is one of the most potent factors in human achievement. It refers to enthusiasm and passion for something or someone, a desire to protect it and if necessary sacrifice in its behalf; it means loving what you are doing to such an extent that you insist on its being done the best possible way. The best way, of course, may take considerable time and effort; without commitment this expenditure of time and effort is impossible.

Unfortunately, there are aspects of contemporary American society which seriously undermine impulse control. One of these is the emphasis on consumption. Widespread and continuous consumption is a necessity for the present American economy, and it is stimulated by manufacturers and their agents, the advertisers and mass media. We are constantly urged to buy; in fact, we are urged to *want*, to gratify, to indulge, regardless of need or consequences. The slogan "Buy now, pay later" sums up the whole process appallingly well—it is also a very good description of lack of impulse control. The old Protestant ethic, with its emphasis on waiting and denial of present satisfaction (all too often carried to an unhealthy and destructive extreme) has given way to its opposite, an ethic of perpetual ingestion. Moreover, to keep us consuming at a profitable rate, manufacturers utilize "built-in obsolescence" in easily breakable mechanical devices and constantly changing fashions. This phenomenon has become a psychological fact of contemporary life, and has significant ramifications. The concept of built-in obsolescence extends beyond objects to works of art and to people themselves, so that only what is new (or young) is considered valuable, and adults are as much caught up in this attitude as are young people.

Self-control need not be an agony of renunciation. But children must learn about cause and effect—that if they do something, other things will happen as a result. This knowledge is essential for ordering and partially controlling reality with judgment and prediction. Failure to use these tools represents a reversion to infantilism and magical thinking ("I will be taken care of regardless of what happens"), a belief in one's personal dispensation from responsibility.

While they do make some provisions for protection and care-taking, colleges generally operate on the premise that students are responsible, that is, are both in control and answerable. For example, at the Harvard University Health Services, psychiatrists do not intercede on behalf of a student whose actions incur disciplinary measures. It is not the psychiatrist's function to inform deans about infractions of rules, but neither is it his job (nor is it considered therapeutic) to act as *deus ex machina* and rescue (and, by implication, excuse) a student from the consequences of his behavior, even if it is of the psychologically determined or acting-out variety.

Acting out (aggressive antisocial behavior which expresses underlying conflict) is common among adolescents, and is often a transitory phenomenon. Understanding, support, and brief therapy are helpful, but condoning such behavior is not, because it implies that the young person is not being taken seriously and negates the educational process of teaching responsibility and acceptable channeling of antisocial impulses. At times such severe personality disordering may have taken place that the patient is diagnosed as psychotic; such a person, though usually not legally responsible for his behavior, must gradually be led back to assuming full responsibility for himself as his treatment progresses. In the process both he and others may need the protection offered by his removal to a sheltered environment. This procedure is therapeutic, not punitive, and (if possible) the patient should be made aware of this.

Drug-taking is also seen by many students as being a matter of individual decision; however, opposition to it is mainly for medical reasons, not because it is in itself a sign of degeneracy or a cause of severely delinquent behavior. Marijuana is not addicting (although it *is* illegal and sometimes unpleasant), and occasional experiments motivated by normal curiosity or mild rebellion may do little or no damage. Taken continually, it makes effective functioning impossible. LSD, the amphetamines, and the true narcotics are another story, and their use is generally only one of several signs of severe personal difficulties.

Censorship and self-righteous scolding are never effective with young people, especially in the fact of peer group pressures. Reasoned discussions in which facts and informed opinion are honestly expressed and which leave students free to make their own decisions are necessary. No matter how much teachers may wish to "protect" young people and help them avoid what seems like obvious danger, they cannot use force of any kind without students' reading their efforts (perhaps quite rightly) as both authoritarian and condescending; moreover, they may confirm a student's belief in the rightness of his behavior and increase its efficacy as a means of protest. (I am not referring here to illegal actions, which present a relatively clear-cut situation, but to those less well-defined areas involving personal judgment.) Sometimes errors are quite expensive; nonetheless, hand-me-down attitudes and a heavy-handed approach deprive the student of experience as an educational tool and of the freedom of choice—including his own freedom to make mistakes. Students can gain a great deal simply from knowing that teachers are sincerely concerned with their welfare, i.e., that teachers' opinions about right behavior pertain to the students' best interests and are not merely reflections of a personal stake in maintaining authority.

Young people's advocacy of new attitudes and values expresses their belief in the discovery of new ways of thinking and talking about man, and their awareness of elements in traditional moral-ity which no longer serve a useful purpose, rather than a total relinquishing of moral and ethical considerations. The fundamental principles are of the primacy of internal controls, individually relevant situations, and emphasis on the human personalities, rather than *a priori* standards. People of college age tend to be more adventurous, intense, radical, impulsive, and idealistic than adults; that this is true has many implications (some of which I have discussed above) for their "caretakers." The fundamental one, I think, is that we try to demonstrate and exemplify the values of education for them because we believe that *they* are valuable. Like parents, we want to pass on the good things and help our heirs to be the kind of people who can make the best use of them. Moreover, we should always be aware that college students are important as much for what they are as for what they will become. A girl at Barnard College said, "I'm just sick and tired of being potential all the time." While it is true that young people are on the road, that road is itself a place.

## REFERENCES

1. "Student Protests: A Phenomenon for Behavioral Sciences Research," *Science* (161:3836), July 5, 1968, pp. 20-22.
2. *Crisis at Columbia,* Cox Commission Report: Report of the Fact-Finding Commission to Investigate the Disturbances at Columbia University in April and May 1968. New York: Vintage Books, 1968;

   A. C. Eurich, ed. *Campus 1980,* New York: Delacorte Press, 1968;

   L. S. Feuer, *The Conflict of Generations,* New York: Basic Books, 1969;

   G. F. Kennan, *Democracy and the Student Left,* Boston: Atlantic, Little Brown, 1968;

   K. Keniston, *The Uncommitted,* New York: Harcourt, Brace & World, 1965;

   ———, *The Young Radicals,* New York: Harcourt, Brace & World, 1968;

S. M. Lipset and S. S. Wolin, *The Berkeley Student Revolt,* Garden City, New York: Anchor Books, 1965;

D. Mallery, *Ferment on the Campus,* New York: Harper and Row, 1966;

N. Sanford, *Where Colleges Fail,* San Francisco: Jossey-Bass, Inc., 1967.

3. C. Frankel, in *Dilemmas of Youth,* R. M. MacIver, ed., published by the Institute for Religious and Social Studies, distributed by Harper and Brothers, New York: 1961, pp. 66-67.

4. Anne Chamberlin, "King of Supershape," *Esquire,* January 1966, p. 113.

5. E. Erikson, *Childhood and Society,* 2nd ed., New York: W. W. Norton, 1963.

6. ———, "Youth and the Life Cycle," *Children,* 7:44-45, March-April 1960.

7. Ibid. p. 48.

8. Harvard *Crimson* Commencement Supplement, 1966, pp. 7, 22.

9. Ibid.

# The National Assessment of Educational Progress: Issues and Problems*

## ARNO A. BELLACK

Interstate commerce in educational goals is not forbidden—the schools of all the states share common purposes.

Most of the influences that are decisively shaping the instructional programs of the American schools in the present era are not local, but national in scope and character. The march of events in the nation and in the world is placing extraordinary demands on our schools—demands to equalize educational opportunity for all the nation's children, to provide quality teaching for all students, and to make certain that we have an adequate national supply of trained manpower.

Federal support is here to stay. If the educational profession and interested citizens are to influence the direction in which national policies for education are to move, we need more accurate information about what is going on in the schools; we need to identify aspects of the instructional program in which improvement is needed. We need to assess on a nationwide basis the progress we have made and proceed to work out national educational policies designed to carry out the commitments we share.

## I. Introduction

The growing national stake in education is evident in the great variety of educational activities currently sponsored by numerous governmental and non-governmental agencies operating at the national level. Impressed by the growing importance of education for every aspect of our national life, and disturbed by the difficulty of making decisions about educational matters without

* Adapted from a paper read at the 1966 meeting of the American Educational Research Association.

dependable data about what our schools are actually accomplish-
ing in terms of student learning, the Carnegie Corporation in
1964 appointed an Exploratory Committee on Assessing the
Progress of Education under the chairmanship of Ralph Tyler
to consider the feasibility of launching an assessment program
to measure our educational achievements on a national scale.
Plans for the national assessment drawn up by the Exploratory
Committee have been described in articles in various educational
periodicals.[1]

Since the assessment calls for the participation of the nation's
schools in an activity never before undertaken, we would do
well to examine carefully the problems and issues raised by the
proposal. I shall discuss two issues that seem to me to be crucial:
(1) the probable influence of the assessment on the curricula
of the nation's schools, and (2) the proposed procedures for
selecting the objectives for the assessment—that is, the way in
which decisions are to be made regarding *what* is to be evaluated.

## II. Influence of the Assessment on the Curriculum

In discussing the probable influences of the proposed national
assessment on the curriculum, we do well to keep in mind Lee
Cronbach's reminder that it was for purposes of curriculum
improvement that systematic evaluation was first introduced.
He points out that "When that famous muckraker Joseph Rice
gave the same spelling test in a number of American schools,
and so gave the first impetus to the educational testing movement, he was interested in evaluating a curriculum. Crusading
against the extended spelling drills that then loomed large in the
school schedule—'the spelling grind'—Rice collected evidence of
their worthlessness so as to provoke curriculum revision."[2]

There are many indications that we are returning to this view
that the improvement of curriculum and instruction is a significant function of evaluation, after a period in which evaluation
was used primarily for making decisions about individual
students and for administrative assessment of teachers and school

systems.[3] For example, Jerome Bruner in his recent book, *Toward a Theory of Instruction,* suggests that we view evaluation as "a form of educational intelligence for the guidance of curriculum construction and pedagogy."[4] The purpose of an assessment program, in this view, is not to condemn or to praise, not to compare one course with another or one teacher with another, not to pit one school's curriculum against another school's curriculum. Rather, as Cronbach suggests, the most important service evaluation can perform is to identify aspects of the instructional program in which improvement is needed.[5]

To the present time there has been no attempt to assess, for purposes of curriculum improvement, the educational performance of American schools on a national scale. And the reasons are not difficult to find. Even efforts to evaluate specific curricula that carry students through a major part of their school years— what John Carroll calls "school learning over the long haul"— present great technical difficulties and have rarely been undertaken in any systematic way.

Given the technical problems involved, it is not at all strange that no effort has been made to assess the results of schooling on a national basis. Equally important, however, and just as inhibiting, have been traditionally held notions regarding the locus of responsibility for determining instructional policies and programs. The "conventional wisdom" of educators and laymen has long held that curriculum improvement, including the evaluation of instruction, is the exclusive prerogative of local and state school systems. Interestingly enough, educators have not hesitated to propose objectives for *all* the nation's elementary and secondary schools. Witness, for example, the two studies sponsored by the Russell Sage Foundation outlining behavioral objectives for both elementary and secondary schools.[6] There is no hint in these reports that interstate commerce in educational goals is forbidden, that objectives for the schools dare not cross state lines. Indeed, the assumption in these studies, and in numerous others, is that the schools of all the states do in fact share common purposes. But in the past, suggestions that we assess the progress of our nation's schools in terms of these common objectives have not been made; and if such proposals had been made, it is safe to say that they would have been rejected out of hand.

In current debates about the proposed national assessment, the conventional wisdom long honored in educational circles about the exclusive responsibility of local and state school systems for curriculum improvement and the assessment of educational outcomes is being called into question. The enemy of the conventional wisdom, John Galbraith tells us, is the march of events. The fatal blow comes when conventional ideas fail to deal with new conditions and problems to which obsolescence has made them clearly inapplicable. The march of events in the nation and in the world is placing extraordinary demands on our schools—demands to equalize educational opportunity for all the nation's children, to provide quality teaching for all students, and to make certain that we have an adequate national supply of trained manpower. These demands are forcing us to reexamine our instructional programs and the institutional arrangements at local, state, and national levels through which we formulate curriculum policies and assess our progress.

In his 1965 Horace Mann Lecture, Lawrence Cremin argued, quite rightly I think, that most of the influences that are decisively shaping the instructional programs of the American schools in the present era are not local, but national in scope and character.[7] The responses on the part of governmental and non-governmental agencies concerned with education have likewise been national in scope. Witness, for example, the programs for curriculum improvement under the auspices of the federal government. The National Science Foundation has led in the reform of curricula in the sciences and social sciences throughout the nation's schools. Through its varied programs of research and development, the U.S. Office of Education has sponsored projects in mathematics, English, social studies, and science. In addition, the Office has allocated large sums of money to improve the curricula for disadvantaged students and for vocational training. Equally important are nationwide non-governmental influences on the curriculum. The National Education Association through its Project on Instruction identified critical curriculum problems and issues faced by American schools and formulated recommendations for dealing with them. The professional organizations of many of the scholarly disciplines—economics, biology, mathematics, anthropology, and geography, to name just a few—have mounted major efforts directed toward the improvement of teaching in the schools. Foundations like Ford and Carnegie have funded projects undertaken by universities and school systems to improve classroom instruction throughout the country.

All of these efforts at instructional improvement are national in scope and character. In spite of a continuing emphasis on local responsibility for curriculum planning, we have developed what is in effect a loosely-knit national framework within which curriculum improvement now proceeds. What has evolved is not a centralized authority capable of introducing a standardized, national curriculum in every elementary and secondary school in the nation. Indeed, in many subject areas there are competing programs, each committed to a different approach to teaching. With few exceptions, the focus of attention in each of the curriculum improvement projects is an individual discipline; little or no attention is given to the relationships of the teaching fields to each other, or to the program of studies within which the various subjects must find their place.

Within this loosely-knit national framework, many assume that the national interests in education will be best served by the efforts of each school and school district to work out its own curriculum salvation, drawing on a variety of sources for help, including the numerous competing national projects. But many citizens and educators are convinced that this approach will result neither in widespread improvement of the quality of teaching nor in equalization of educational opportunity for all youth—goals to which the entire nation is committed. They urge that we frankly acknowledge the need to assess on a nationwide basis the progress we have made and proceed to work out national educational policies designed to carry out the commitments we share as a nation.

In the development of national policies it seems reasonable to assume that the federal government will play an important, but not exclusive role. We have already noted that the national interest in education has called forth new programs of federal assistance for the schools, including support for curriculum improvement. Equally important has been the influence of the federal courts in shaping educational policy through Supreme Court decisions on such matters as racial segregation and religion in the schools. Under these circumstances, as the Rockefeller Report on Education suggests, "it is important for those who are apprehensive about the growth of federal support of education to examine the *direction* which it takes. There is no chance that we can turn back the clock and eliminate federal support of education. There is a chance that farsighted men may influence the *direction* of federal support or the *kinds* of federal support."[8]

If the profession and interested citizens are to influence the direction in which national policies for education are to move, we need more accurate information about what is going on in the schools. We need to assess our schools to determine what the curriculum needs are and where instructional improvements must be undertaken. It seems clear that an assessment program such as that proposed by Carnegie's Exploratory Committee would provide us with vitally needed information of this kind. It is, therefore, disconcerting to note that virtually no attention has been given by the supporters of the assessment plan to its function in improving instruction in our schools. It is the critics of the proposal who have raised the issue of the assessment's probable influence on the curriculum. There are those, for example, who fear that the assessment program is actually the camel's nose under the tent and that the inevitable result will be a standardized, national curriculum.[9] Proponents of the plan frequently respond with assurances that teaching for the tests and revising curricula to conform to test content will not be stimulated because of the design of the instruments and the sampling procedures to be followed. It seems strange indeed to hear proponents of the assessment assert that it will be the "fault" not of national assessors, but of curriculum builders, if the assessment does in fact influence curriculum policies.

To give assurance that the assessment program is not designed to influence the instructional programs of our schools is to deny what is one of the most significant functions of any assessment, namely, to identify aspects of the curriculum where improvement is needed. If the results of the appraisal do in fact reveal the extent to which students at various ages are or are not achieving important learning objectives, then it is not at all unreasonable to argue that the results should indeed influence curriculum planning. The significant question, it seems to me, is not whether the results of the assessment will influence the curriculum (they are bound to do so in any event), but rather how the results can be wisely used in the service of instructional improvement, by whom, in conjunction with what other kinds of evidence, and at what levels in the organizational structure of the nation's schools. In the debate now getting underway about the merits and shortcomings of the proposed national assessment, we would do well to deal forthrightly with these questions if the assessment is to be used in the service of curriculum improvement.

Equally important, we should recognize that if our primary goal is curriculum improvement, it will be necessary to parallel the assessment program with research efforts that will result in knowledge about factors in the school environment (such as teaching methods, materials, and administrative arrangements) and community factors (such as the level of financial support and citizen interest) that influence educational outcomes. For without knowledge about relevant school and community factors, the results of assessment provide only a partial basis for curriculum development activities aimed at improving educational outcomes.

Furthermore, new patterns of cooperation among local, state, and national levels of school organization are clearly needed to carry on the assessment and to support essential research and development activities. What is called for, obviously, is not replacing exclusive local and state responsibility for the assessment and for curriculum research and development with exclusive federal responsibility. For, as John Fischer has cautioned us, we ought not to attempt to settle difficult, complex educational problems by generalized appeals to the virtue of a particular level of control. Rather, what is called for is the development of new patterns of local, state, and federal responsibility and control such as those recently recommended by Roald Campbell, John Fischer, James Conant, and Francis Keppel.[10] At this point, I am not arguing for any one of these approaches; rather, my contention is that new patterns of collaboration must be built if we are to benefit from the results of the assessment.


## III. Selection of Objectives for the Assessment

One of the most difficult tasks facing the group responsible for planning the assessment is that of determining the objectives to be appraised. Although discussions about goals and purposes fill volumes in education libraries, we have only a limited number of adequately developed theories for the derivation and validation of objectives.


### PROCEDURES FOR SELECTION

For purposes of the assessment it is, of course, necessary to define the goals to be appraised in behavioral terms that permit their observation and measurement. The framework for the selection of objectives has been set by seven areas that are labeled "important educational tasks of the modern school": reading and language arts, science, mathematics, social studies, citizenship, fine arts, and vocational education. It is significant that the Exploratory Committee chose not to begin, as might have been anticipated, with broad general goals, but rather with the identification of what they considered to be major teaching fields. They first raised the question, "What teaching fields should be included in the curriculum?" and then proceeded to identify objectives within each of the seven areas of instruction.

Once the framework has been set by these seven instructional areas, the next major task is that of selecting objectives in each of the areas. The method to be followed is described by Ralph Tyler as follows (I quote at some length because I want to comment on the procedures, and it is important to have them clearly in mind if my comments are to be meaningful):

> In each field, scholars, teachers, and curriculum specialists are formulating statements of the objectives which faithfully reflect the contributions of that field and which the schools are seriously seeking to attain. For each of these major objectives, prototype exercises are being constructed, which, in the opinion of the scholars and teachers, give students an opportunity to demonstrate the behavior implied by the objective. These lists of objectives, and prototype exercises which help to define them are being reviewed by a series of panels composed of public spirited citizens. Each panel will spend two days reviewing the material and assuring themselves that they understand the kind of educational achievement which is described. The panels are also asked to judge each objective as it is stated and defined by the prototype items in terms of the question: 'Is this something important for people to learn today? Is it something I would like to have my children learn?' This process will result in revisions of the original listing of objectives, some of which may be eliminated. However, the procedure is designed to insure that every objective being assessed is considered important by scholars, is accepted as an educational task by the school, and is deemed desirable by leading lay citizens. This should help to eliminate the criticism frequently directed at current tests in which some item is attacked by the scholar as representing shoddy scholarship or criticized by school people as something not in the curriculum, or by prominent laymen as being unimportant or technical trivia.

In working out the composition of the lay panels, John Tukey, member of the Advisory Committee on the project, suggested a plan which deals directly with differences among various sections of the country and various kinds of communities. Following his proposal, four groups of panels will be used to represent four sections of the country, Northeast, South, Midwest and Far West. For each section, three panels will be set up, for communities in rural areas, suburban areas, and cities. Each of the 12 panels will review the lists of objectives and prototoypes and judge them from the background of their experience. Finally, the chairman of the 12 panels will prepare the report on the achievement to be assessed in the national, periodic study of educational progress. . . . *I believe that the decision by the lay panels provides a proper means for selecting the objectives to be appraised in a national assessment even if the panels should consider unimportant certain objectives recommended by scholars.* (italics added) From my experience in talking about such matters with thoughtful citizens, I have come to believe that they will not lightly dismiss recommendations from the scholars and the schools, so that the eliminations will probably be few. More commonly, the lay panels will help to word the objectives and to revise prototypes so that they are clearer and more understandable to laymen.[11]

ANALYSIS OF PROCEDURES

The definition of objectives for public institutions like the schools is far from a simple task, and the procedure just described calls our attention to some of the difficulties involved.

There is general agreement that final responsibility for decisions regarding general goals lies with the public, and this means that decisions about the overall aims of education must work their way through the political process. It is also generally agreed that professional educators require a degree of autonomy in making educational decisions that require expert knowledge and skill. Clearly there is a difference between the domain of public concern and the domain of professional concern. But these domains are ill-defined, and generally accepted criteria are not at hand by which to identify the spheres of professional responsibility on the one hand and the spheres of citizen responsibility on the other. Lacking such criteria, views regarding the allocation of professional and citizen responsibilities inevitably reflect individual biases.

My own biases lead me to question whether citizens can make the final decisions regarding objectives in the subject areas, as proposed by those who have planned the assessment procedures, without interfering in matters that require professional competence. Whether citizens should be the final arbiters in specifying objectives within subject matter areas is admittedly a debatable issue, but I think it is fair to say that a substantial body of professional and lay opinion would seriously question the wisdom of such a procedure. James B. Conant, for example, suggests that "details of course content and choice of textbooks" should be in the hands of professional educators. He writes: "Neither school board members nor other laymen should become involved in the *details* of course content or the choice of textbooks. These, too, are professional matters, except insofar as they may affect the budget. In particular, controversial issues in regard to the specifics of course content should be resolved by professional educators at the elementary, secondary, and university levels."[12]

A somewhat different point of view on this issue is presented by Myron Lieberman in his book *Education as a Profession*.[13] He holds that the American people are in substantial agreement that the purposes of education should include the development of critical thinking, effective communication, creative skills, and social, civic, and occupational competence. According to his view, it is the teaching profession's responsibility to translate these broad purposes into intermediate instructional objectives that serve as the basis for building a coherent educational program, including selection of school subjects and methods of teaching them. Lieberman further proposes that these intermediate objectives might well serve as the basis for evaluating progress made by the profession.

Now whether one agrees with Conant (who would give citizens a role in deciding what subjects to teach, but would leave the teaching of them to professionals) or with Lieberman (who would assign to the teaching profession responsibility for determining both the subjects to be taught and the methods of teaching them), he is led to the conclusion that working out the details of instruction within the subject fields, including the selection of objectives, should be left to the profession. If one accepts either of these viewpoints, it is difficult to subscribe to the procedure to be followed in the assessment which gives laymen the final word in deciding what teaching objectives are appropriate in mathematics, science, and the other subject fields. What if a substantial number of citizen panel members object to the discussion of competing economic systems and political ideologies in the social studies program? Or to the study of human reproduction in science? How many negative votes will force exclusion of a given objective proposed for consideration by the teachers and subject matter specialists? To require citizens to make decisions that require expert knowledge of the field and background in teaching is to invite lay interference in matters that ought to be left in the hands of professionals. It would be unfortunate indeed if the assessment program were to set a precedent for such involvement by laymen in curriculum planning. So I would argue, at any rate.

## IV. Conclusion

In brief, I would contend that, instead of avoiding the question of the influence of the assessment on the instructional programs of the nation's schools, we would do well to encourage widespread debate on the issues involved; and that we begin to work out new patterns of relationships among local, state, and national levels of school government, making certain that the legitimate interests of all three levels are taken into account in developing and carrying out school policies, including those related to assessing the progress of education and improving curricula.

Further, I would suggest that within the framework of the assessment as planned the objectives to be used as the basis of the assessment should be viewed as intermediate objectives, in the sense that Lieberman uses the term, with their determination the responsibility of professional educators, not of laymen. The appropriate role of laymen within this approach is either (1) identification of major teaching fields to be included in the curriculum, or, (2) determination of the broad goals of education on the basis of which the professionals develop intermediate objectives that provide direction for their efforts in the classroom. Acceptance of this point of view does not mean an attitude of "the public be damned." Rather, it recognizes areas of decisions reserved for professionals because of their expert knowledge and skill.

## REFERENCES

1. See, for example, R. Tyler, "Assessing the Progress of Education," *Phi Delta Kappan,* September 1965, pp. 13-16;
   "The Gross Educational Product: How Much are Students Learning?" *Carnegie Quarterly,* Carnegie Corporation of New York, Spring 1966;
   J. Goodlad, "Assessment of Educational Performance," *Contemporary Issues of American Education,* Washington, D.C.: Department of Health, Education, and Welfare, 1965, pp. 33-41.
2. L. Cronbach, "Evaluation for Course Improvement," in R. W. Heath, ed., *New Curricula,* New York: Harper & Row, 1964, pp. 232-233.
3. Ibid.
4. J. Bruner, *Toward a Theory of Instruction,* Cambridge, Mass.: Harvard University Press, 1966, p. 163.
5. L. Cronbach, op. cit. p. 236.
6. N. Kearney, *Elementary School Objectives,* New York: Russell Sage Foundation, 1953, and W. French and Assoc., *Behavioral Goals of General Education in High School,* New York: Russell Sage Foundation, 1957.
7. L. Cremin, *The Genius of American Education,* Pittsburgh: University of Pittsburgh Press, 1965, p. 100.
8. *The Pursuit of Excellence, The Rockefeller Report in Education,* New York: Doubleday, 1958, p. 35.

9. See H. Hand, "National Assessment Viewed as the Camel's Nose," *Phi Delta Kappan*, September 1965, pp. 8-13.

10. See R. Campbell and G. Sroufe, "Toward a Rationale for Federal-State-Local Relations in Education," *Phi Delta Kappan*, September 1965, pp. 2-7;

J. Fischer, "The Question of Control," New York: Teachers College, 1966;

J. Conant, *Shaping Educational Policy*, New York: McGraw-Hill, 1964;

F. Keppel, *The Necessary Revolution in American· Education*, New York: Harper & Row, 1966.

11. Ralph W. Tyler, "The Development of Instruments for Assessing Educational Progress," *Proceedings of the 1965 Invitational Conference on Testing Problems*, Princeton, N.J.: Educational Testing Service, 1965, pp. 97-98.

12. J. B. Conant, *Education in the Junior High School Years*, Princeton, N.J.: Educational Testing Service, 1960, p. 14.

13. M. Lieberman, *Education as a Profession*, Englewood Cliffs, N.J.: Prentice-Hall, 1956.

# The Impact of Collective Negotiations on American Education*

### MICHAEL H. MOSKOW

"Collective negotiations" is a process whereby the employees in a school district collectively choose an organization to represent them. This organization then meets with the school board or the school board representative to determine jointly the salaries and conditions of employment of the employees. Hopefully the parties will make proposals and counter-proposals in good faith and eventually reach an agreement.

This is bilateral decision-making as opposed to unilateral decision-making. It is quite different from just giving the employees an opportunity to make proposals or even consulting with them before the school board makes a decision. In effect, collective negotiations is an agreement-making process.

There is no question that an increasing number of school boards will negotiate with teacher organizations in future years. The final impact on the education of our children will depend on how educational leaders guide and use the collective negotiations movement.

## I. Introduction and Background

Aside from the controversial nature of this subject, there is a serious semantic problem in talking about negotiations in public education. The problem arises in part because of the intense competition between the National Education Association and the American Federation of Teachers. The NEA refers to its approach to teacher negotiations as "professional negotiation";

* For a further elaboration of many of the ideas expressed in this paper see *Collective Negotiations for Teachers: An Approach to School Administration* by Myron Lieberman and Michael H. Moskow, New York: Rand McNally and Company, 1966, and *Teachers and Unions* by Michael H. Moskow, Philadelphia: University of Pennsylvania Press, 1966.

the AFT uses the term "collective bargaining." Unfortunately, a great deal of antagonism has built up between these two competing teacher organizations, especially when representation elections are conducted in school districts.

As a result, I have found that whenever I use the term "professional negotiation," AFT supporters usually close their ears; on the other hand, when I use the term "collective bargaining," it is the NEA supporters who rarely listen to what I say. Actually, I do not see too much difference between the two approaches; in fact, the great variety among the local affiliates of each organization makes any ideological differences existing on the national level even less meaningful. Therefore, I use the term "collective negotiations" in referring to the approaches of both teacher organizations. Hopefully, this will enable us to discuss the problems in a more objective fashion.

The NEA has a membership of over 1,000,000 consisting of classroom teachers, school administrators, college professors, college administrators, and specialists in schools, colleges, and educational agencies which are both public and private. Classroom teachers in public schools constitute over 85 per cent of the total membership. One of the major beliefs of the NEA, however, is that since education is a profession unique unto itself, membership in associations should not be limited to classroom teachers. Therefore, all state affiliates and most local associations accept both teachers and administrators as members.

In line with its concept of professionalism, the NEA uses the term "professional negotiation" to distinguish its effort at bargaining from the traditional collective bargaining procedures of the labor movement. When an impasse arises, it advocates various forms of third party intervention, most of which consist of modified forms of mediation and fact finding. At no time, however, will it advocate using the services of state labor relations agencies or state mediation agencies since, in NEA's opinion, disputes should always be settled through "educational channels." In extreme cases, when agreement cannot be reached, the Association will resort to sanctions which may range from publicizing unfavorable teaching conditions in a particular school district to a mass refusal to sign contracts by all teachers employed in the district.

As would be expected, the AFT makes no effort to distinguish its approach to teacher-board relations from traditional collective bargaining. Although it does not advocate strikes as a means of settling impasses, the 1963 national convention passed a resolution which recognized the right of locals to strike under certain circumstances and urged ". . . the AFL-CIO and affiliated international unions to support such strikes when they occur." This resolution constituted a change in AFT policy, since in prior years there had been no official strike policy even though locals had been supported when they went on strike.

Nationally, the AFT has over 140,000 members with the majority of their membership concentrated in large cities. The constitution grants locals the right to determine on an individual basis whether or not administrators shall be admitted as members; but few administrators join, and often they are prohibited from holding office or even voting on motions. Thus, the AFT emphasizes that it is the only organization specifically devoted to the interests of classroom teachers.

Although the NEA and the AFT have been competing since 1919, the struggle gained new impetus in December 1961 when the United Federation of Teachers, a local affiliate of the AFT, was elected bargaining agent for 44,000 New York City public school teachers. The UFT received nearly three times as many votes as the NEA's hastily formed contender—the Teachers Bargaining Organization. More important, though, was the fact that for the first time the labor movement gave active support, in the form of personnel and financial resources, to a local of the AFT. Shortly after the victory, the AFT joined the Industrial Union Department of the AFL-CIO which had been the major contributor to the UFT. Since that time, the IUD, headed by Walter Reuther, has been deeply involved in helping the AFT organize public school teachers and conduct campaigns for collective bargaining. The AFT has won collective bargaining rights for teachers in Boston, Detroit, Cleveland, Philadelphia, Chicago, Hartford, and a number of smaller cities.

No doubt the UFT victory in New York City stimulated other locals of the AFT to press for negotiation rights in order to maintain their leadership position. Full-time IUD organizers were assigned to AFT locals in Philadelphia and Boston after the New York election. The Philadelphia local had approximately 350 members in 1962; two and one-half years later the local was elected bargaining agent to represent over 10,000 public school teachers in Philadelphia. They now claim to have a membership of approximately 4300.

During the above period of time, the NEA was equally active. Six months after the UTF victory in New York City the NEA held its 1962 convention in Denver. Dr. William Carr, Executive Secretary of the NEA, entitled his address "The Turning Point," which I feel aptly describes the dramatic changes that took place in the NEA policy toward collective negotiations at this convention. First, they passed their official resolution on "professional negotiations." This was the first time that the term "negotiations" was used by the NEA. In previous years, they had used terms such as "cooperative determination," "collective determination," and even "democratic persuasion."

Second, they adopted an official policy on "professional sanctions" which has been used several times in local school districts and twice on a statewide basis—in Utah in 1964 and recently in the state of Oklahoma. One of the techniques the NEA used in Oklahoma was to establish placement centers to help Oklahoma teachers find jobs in other states.

Third, Carr identified teacher unionism as one of the two major crises in education and formed the Urban Project to meet the needs of large-city teachers and to direct the NEA's battle with the AFT. The changing expenditure pattern of the Urban Project demonstrates its growing importance in the NEA. In 1961-1962 the Urban Project spent a total of $28,000. In 1962-1963 their budget was over $203,000, while in 1964-1965 the Urban Project spent over $884,000 out of a total NEA budget of approximately $10,000,000.

In many respects changes were made at the 1965 NEA convention which were even more significant than the ground-breaking steps taken in 1962. The NEA strengthened its resolution on sanctions and the last paragraph of their resolution on "professional negotiations" which had been passed at the 1962 convention. The paragraph had read:

> The resolution of differences between professional associations and boards of education must be provided for in such a manner as to preclude the arbitrary exercise of unilateral authority by boards of education and the use of the strike by teachers.[1]

The word "strike" was taken out of this resolution, and it now reads:

> The seeking of consensus and mutual agreement on a professional basis should preclude the arbitrary exercise of unilateral authority by boards of education, administrators, or teachers.[2]

Notice that administrators are now included in the resolution with teachers and school boards.

Another development of the 1965 convention was the passing of a resolution directing the executive committee:

> The seeking of consensus and mutual agreement on a professional basis should preclude the arbitrary exercise of unilateral action by boards of education, administrators, or teachers.[3]

No doubt, this resolution was passed at least in part in response to AFT allegations that the NEA is dominated by administrators and not responsive to the wishes of the classroom teachers.

Finally, 1965 was the year in which the Executive Committee of the NEA approved its revised *Guidelines for Professional Negotiations*.[4] In my opinion there are two major changes in the revised *Guidelines*. First, the NEA now strongly advocates exclusive recognition whereby one organization represents all teachers in a district regardless of whether or not all teachers are members of this organization. Under the old *Guidelines* the NEA accepted any kind of representation system and called it "professional negotiation."

Another major change is that the NEA now strongly advocates the adoption of written agreements which include any terms and conditions of employment that have been negotiated by a local teacher organization and its board of education. Prior to 1965, the NEA had accepted many different types of professional negotiation agreements. Now they are placing great emphasis on including the terms and conditions of employment in the written agreement that would be signed by both the teacher organization leaders and the school board president. There is no question that both of these changes indicate a much greater sophistication on the part of the NEA toward collective negotiations.

As far as state association policies toward collective negotiations are concerned, a wide variety of approaches has developed. Some state associations have been moving very rapidly; others have not moved at all. It is certainly significant, however, that in 1965 fifteen state education associations sponsored legislation which would have required boards of education to negotiate with designated teacher organizations. In prior years only two teacher organizations ever sponsored legislation of this type.

Eight states have enacted negotiation statutes up to this date: California, Connecticut, Massachusetts, Michigan, Oregon, Rhode Island, Washington, and Wisconsin. The major significance of these laws is that prior to 1965 only one state, Wisconsin, had a statute which required school boards to negotiate with designated teacher organizations. Now there are eight states in this category.

## II. What Is "Collective Negotiations"?

Before discussing the impact of collective negotiations on American education, it is necessary to define the term, since confusion over the precise meaning has caused many unnecessary controversies and differences of opinion. Collective negotiations is a process whereby the employees in a school district collectively choose an organization to represent them.

This organization then meets with the school board or the school board representative to determine jointly the salaries and conditions of employment of the employees. The parties, it is hoped, will make proposals and counterproposals in good faith and eventually reach an agreement. This is a bilateral decision-making process as opposed to unilateral decision-making. It is quite different from just giving the employees an opportunity to make proposals or even consulting with them before the school board makes a decision. In effect, collective negotiations is an agreement-making process.

When the school board and teacher organization reach agreement on salaries and conditions of employment, the terms are offered to each individual teacher in the same way this would be done without collective negotiations. Each teacher may then accept or reject the jointly determined terms of employment and accept a job in another school district if he sees fit. The school board, on the other hand, passes a resolution establishing the jointly determined terms of employment as its official policy. Thus, in order for negotiations to be successful, it is necessary for the school board to give to its negotiators a set of parameters within which they will accept a settlement.

## III. Why Teacher Militancy?

In order for school boards to deal effectively with teacher organizations, they must have some understanding of the reason for the recent increase in teacher militancy. Like any good academician, I can give at least ten different causes for this phenomenon.

Basically, there are three different areas of *potential* conflict in any school system. First, there is a possible conflict over the allocation of funds to public education. Teachers usually want higher salaries, and in some cases they want more funds allocated to education in general. The attitude of the community, on the other hand, may vary from a willingness to spend more on public education to a strong resistance to any further increases in the funds allocated. In any community, there are always some groups of citizens who are attempting to keep education costs as low as possible.

The position of the school board will vary among different communities. In some cases, the board will side with those who want to minimize expenditures on education, and in other cases the board will side with the teachers and other groups that want to increase expenditures. Their position will depend on a number of different variables, but in large part it will depend on the pressures placed on the board by the community at large and by various groups of citizens.

Second, there is a potential conflict over the rules that govern the employment relationship of the teacher. On matters such as class size, number of teaching assignments, class schedules, seniority, and transfer plans, the superintendent often wants to maintain a degree of flexibility. Teachers, on the other hand, usually want protection from any arbitrary or discriminatory application of the rules.

A third area of potential conflict occurs over the professional function of the teacher. In public education there is a large group of professionals working for a common employer. Since professional workers are often confronted with a wide variety of problems which require the application of a high degree of intelligence and specialized training, it is essential that they have a broad range of autonomy. Thus, professional employees will seek greater control over their jobs and a share in the decision-making that affects them. Our system of lay control of public education almost necessitates a conflict between professionally trained teachers and lay boards of education on matters such as curricula, textbooks, homework, teaching machines, and audio-visual aids.

Even though the above three areas of potential conflict have existed in public education for many years, teachers have recently displayed greater militancy and have attempted to persuade school boards to negotiate with them on the terms and conditions of their employment. Several factors which explain in part this recent change can be identified.

First, as part of its attempts to organize white-collar workers, the labor movement has given active support to the American Federation of Teachers in its drive to unionize teachers. In addition to giving financial support, the Industrial Union Department of the AFL-CIO has full-time organizers working with AFT locals. Second, the consolidation of school districts and the intensified problems of large city teaching have most likely added to the pressures for more effective teacher organizations.

Third, the increase in the percentage of our labor force working as government employees has caused a general drive for negotiation procedures for all public employees. Fourth, as the percentage of male teachers increases and turnover rates among teachers decrease, there is some evidence that a greater career commitment results. Finally, the intense competition between the NEA and the AFT could be contributing to teacher militancy.

## IV. The Impact of Collective Negotiations on Teacher Organizations

Collective negotiations will result in a substantial increase in the number of full-time teacher organization leaders at the local level. This will occur for a number of reasons. Assuming that a substantial number of local affiliates are negotiating with their school boards, it will soon become impossible for a national organization to have its field staff service these local organizations. Furthermore, not only are negotiations usually too time consuming to be conducted by a person who has a full-time teaching job, but it is also disadvantageous to the teachers in terms of effective representation. In small school districts, teacher organizations will most likely join together to hire full-time staff members to service small districts.

Full-time local staff members will have a definite effect upon local teacher organizations. Aside from substantial increases in local organization dues, the most obvious result will be more effective representation of teacher interests at the local level. In fact, full-time local executive secretaries will want to make every attempt to satisfy their members in order to keep their jobs. Thus they will have a vested interest in more effective representation for teachers.

The full-time local leader will also make teacher organizations more active politically at the local level. Although local teacher organizations have recently showed signs of becoming interested in local politics, the growth in the number of full-time leaders will no doubt greatly accentuate this trend.

Finally, the increase in this new breed of local leaders will cause a change in the power structure of teacher organizations. In the past, state education associations have maintained a very powerful position in the NEA. The growth of full-time local leaders means that local associations will have an organizational base to challenge the leadership of the state organizations. This is likely to have a salutary effect on state leadership, especially where such leadership has not been under much pressure to achieve results. The executive secretaries of the state associations are currently the major center of power of the NEA, but full-time local leaders will undoubtedly assume a share of this power.

## V. Organizational Security

Mancur Olson, Jr.[5] has stated that if the benefits a member is to receive are not dependent on his contribution to his organization it is unlikely that he will support the organization. The result is that the organization must find some way of inducing or coercing people into supporting the organization. For example, since all United States citizens receive the benefits of national defense, most citizens would not voluntarily pay to support our armed forces. The result is that citizens are required by law to pay taxes.

The strongest form of organizational security would be a requirement that an employee could not obtain a job unless he is a member of the employee organization. This idea has been modified in different ways in order to guarantee support for employee organizations. Physicians often must be members of county medical associations to get hospital privileges in that county. In over one-half the states, attorneys must belong to state bar associations before they can practice law in that state. Finally, in private industry unions have relied upon the union shop in order to guarantee them support from their constituents.

Up to now, both the National Education Association and the American Federation of Teachers have strongly supported the freedom of any individual teacher to join or refrain from joining a teacher organization. The AFT accuses the NEA of relying upon administrators to coerce teachers into joining the NEA and its affiliates. The NEA accuses the AFT of using various forms of organizational coercion in order to get teachers to join the AFT. These attitudes will no doubt change in a very short period of time.* In fact, if it were not for the rivalry between the two organizations, it is unlikely that they would take their present positions.

An example may help to illustrate this point. In Philadelphia, the Philadelphia Federation of Teachers has the responsibility to negotiate for approximately 10,000 professional employees in the school district. It is also required to represent these employees in the grievance procedure and other matters that may arise in their employment relationship. At present they have approximately 3500 members in this organization. Thus the 3500 members that are supporting the organization pay for the representation of over 10,000 teachers. From an economic point of view, the PFT cannot provide effective representation of all 10,000 teachers unless it has a considerable increase in its membership. The only way that it could increase its membership drastically would be to rely upon some means of coercion or pressure. There is really little incentive for a teacher to join the PFT now, since he is guaranteed the benefits of the organization regardless of whether he joins or not.

* By early 1969 both the AFT and the NEA favored the "agency shop," a form of organizational security. Over two hundred such clauses have been negotiated in the state of Michigan by locals of both organizations.

## VI. Competition Between the NEA and the AFT

The intense and highly spirited competition between the NEA and the AFT has some very important implications for American education. There are, no doubt, some positive aspects to the competition. For example, it may be causing both organizations to be more representative of the interests of their members. In fact, the competition may be causing the rapid growth of the collective negotiations movement. After all, the rapid increase of the NEA interest in professional negotiations seems to have followed rather closely the AFT victory in New York City. On the other hand, enormous amounts of time and money are being spent by the organizations in an effort to denounce the efforts of their rivals. No doubt, more constructive uses could be made of these funds and energies.

The competition also lowers the image of the teacher in the eyes of the public. When the two organizations criticize each other publicly, people are not sure either knows the right way to educate their children. If teaching is ever to be considered a profession, it must have a strong professional organization capable of disciplining its members. How can an organization perform this policing function when it is being challenged by a rival organization and is dependent on voluntary memberships for support?

The negative reaction of each teacher organization to proposals by its opponent also may have some impact on effective representation. The NEA opposes all "labor tactics," yet some tactics used in private industry may be very helpful to teachers. On the other hand, the AFT has never had a strong program of "professional ethics" mainly because the NEA has emphasized this aspect of their program. A blanket statement that everything an opponent does is bad may very possibly result in elimination of some very effective techniques.

Finally, the competition interferes with effective teacher-school board relations. An incumbent organization being challenged by a rival is forced to become more militant and constantly demonstrate it is getting "more" for its members and prospective members. This may be undesirable in many cases since the increased militancy may prevent the school board and teacher organization from developing a sound working relationship.

## VII. The Impact of Collective Negotiations on School Administration

School administrators are deeply concerned about collective negotiations. They are particularly worried about the impact of this new development on their role in the school district and on the performance of their job. Their concern has no doubt led to some unwarranted fears that the teacher organizations will begin to run their school districts. On the other hand, the strong reaction of school administrators may be a sign they recognize the collective negotiations movement is here to stay.

The most immediate impact of collective negotiations will be on school boards and school administrators. For years they have been accustomed to making unilateral decisions on salaries and working conditions of their teachers. They may have asked for recommendations from their teachers, but the ultimate decision was made unilaterally by the school board. Collective negotiations will result in co-determination of these same decisions by teacher organizations and school boards. This will unquestionably place some limits on school administrators and school board members. Although this change from a unilateral decision to a joint decision is taken for granted, individuals are often bewildered once it happens to them. Furthermore, school administrators will be forced to communicate with their teaching staffs through a teacher organization. This will present a new challenge to school administrators accustomed to dealing with teachers on an "individual employee" basis.

The competition between the NEA and AFT may lead some superintendents astray. They may feel that there is some advantage in dealing with one organization or the other. In practice, there is no significant difference between the approaches of the NEA and the AFT in terms of their impact on school administrators. The two organizations certainly have broad ideological differences, but when their policies filter down to the local level, the practical impact is very similar. School administrators have considerable difficulty distinguishing between the "strike" of the AFT and the "professional holiday" of the NEA. In my experience, the same problems arise in negotiations, and the participants usually assume the same roles. In fact, the general tenor of negotiating sessions is very similar.

Superintendents are particularly concerned about what role they should play in collective negotiations. Traditionally the superintendent has been thought of as the executive officer of the school board and the leader of the educational staff. In line with this idea, some superintendents will want to be impartial and perform some kind of fact-finding or fact-supplying function in negotiations. On the other hand, some superintendents will want to assume negotiating responsibility for the school board. The exact role of the superintendent will vary widely among different districts depending on his relationship with his own school board.

In the school districts studied by the author, there was a definite trend for the school board to delegate negotiating responsibility to the superintendent once the board recognized the considerable amount of time that had to be spent in negotiations. In large school districts, the superintendent always had responsibility for directing the negotiating team. At times, board members would attend negotiating sessions, but rarely would they be members of the negotiating team.

Apparently boards of education will often want their superintendents to protect their interests in negotiations. As a result, the superintendent will often be forced to assume overall responsibility for negotiations from the school board point of view. The superintendent will probably not negotiate directly with the teacher organization, since this would be extremely time consuming and no doubt detract from his ability to run the school district. Nevertheless, he will be deeply involved in meeting with the negotiating team and in preparing positions for negotiations.

Principals will also be directly affected by collective negotiations. For example, let us assume that the teacher organization and the school board agree on a clause that limits the number of faculty meetings held in schools to one per month. This will mean that even though principals may feel that two or three faculty meetings are necessary one month and no faculty meetings next month, their flexibility in scheduling faculty meetings will be severely limited. This will no doubt be quite a shock to most principals who are accustomed to a considerable degree of autonomy in making decisions of this type. A wise superintendent will involve his principals in negotiations through a process of consultation or even attendance at negotiating sessions. Even so, however, the discretion of principals and other line supervisors will be limited by collective negotiations.

One final result of collective negotiations will be that many administrators will withdraw from local teacher organizations. This will occur for two reasons. School boards will want to be sure that their superintendents are on their side, while at the same time local teacher organizations will begin to assert their independence and want to become "classroom teacher only" organizations. The following statement by Dr. T. M. Stinnett, a former Assistant Executive Secretary for Professional Development and Welfare of the National Education Association, illustrates this point:

> I do believe that the same lag that has obtained with respect to reapportionment, with the rapid urbanization of the country, has obtained in some NEA policies. I do think that there will result from the current ferment some changes in the role of the superintendent and some modification of the structure of professional organizations. I believe that the role changes will be forced more by school boards than by teachers. There is an evident trend among school boards to insist that the superintendent is exclusively "their man," where professional negotiations agreements are entered into. I believe that, as a result, superintendents may gradually withdraw from inclusive local

associations and the right of voting in local associations. My
guess is that the inclusive local association, excepting the superintendent, will continue but with autonomy for each segment.[6]

It is unlikely that a withdrawal of administrators from local
teacher organizations will result in a complete split of administrators and teachers at all levels in the NEA. They may both
be members of a single national organization, while at the state
level principals and other administrators may want some type
of loose alliance through a confederation of organizations. There
are many different possibilities, but the essential point is that
both teachers and administrators will find that their own interests will be best served through separate organizations.

Evidence that principals are beginning to think of their own
interests in negotiations may be found in two resolutions adopted
by the Michigan Association of Secondary School Principals
in 1965. One resolution urged school districts to recognize bargaining agents for "administrative and supervisory groups which
are excluded by law from the selection of the sole bargaining
agent for teachers." The second resolution urged the Michigan
Education Association "to consider structuring its organization
to provide for completely separate and autonomous departments
of professional personnel which operate under the umbrella
principle of the parent organization."[7]

## VIII. The Economic Impact of Collective Negotiations

One of the most important questions to be answered is whether
collective negotiations will increase the total allocation of funds
to public education. A corollary question is whether teachers'
salaries and expenditures for working conditions will increase
as a result of collective negotiations.

These are not easy questions to answer. In fact, after thirty-
five years of collective bargaining in private employment, there
is still no consensus at to whether unionism and collective

bargaining have caused increases in wages. In public education, however, allocating funds to education is much more of a political decision, and the economic limits of the market place are not present. In my opinon, adding collective negotiations to the present political allocations process will result in increases in total spending for public education. First, collective negotiations will increase the goals and attitudinal favorableness of school boards and school administrators. Second, collective negotiations will increase community support for education because of the increased efforts of a more sophisticated pressure group.

Some persons fear that the increasing power of teachers must cause a decrease in the power of school boards. This analysis, of course, assumes a fixed amount of power in a school system. On the other hand, if the increasing power of teachers results in increased funds allocated to the school board, both the school board and the teachers will increase their power.

If collective negotiations does increase the allocation of funds to education, the results may not be totally beneficial. For example, there are significant differences in spending for public education among different school districts.  In 1965-1966, New York State spent $798, while Mississippi spent only $292 per pupil in average daily attendance. At least part of the above disparity is a result of differences in financial capacity. Thus, if more pressure is applied to wealthy and poor school districts through collective negotiations, the wealthy school districts may get richer and poor school districts may get poorer relatively speaking. (This increasing disparity may result in more federal and state grants to public education.)

## IX. Political Action

Increased political involvement by teachers also appears likely at the local level. Teacher organizations frustrated in negotiations may try to elect school boards and municipal officials more receptive to teacher views. Such efforts are not unusual now, but the advent of collective negotiations will intensify the process. In the past, local teacher organizations have usually been too weak to participate effectively in politics; teacher political involvement at the local level usually emerged from crisis situations. As local teacher organizations achieve a legally protected role in negotiations, they will be forced or pulled into the political arena on a more regular basis. The emergence of full-time local leaders, increased local membership, and higher local dues will increase under the pressure on teacher organizations to participate in local politics and will also increase their ability to do so effectively.

## X. Some Unanswered Questions

The emergence of collective negotiations also poses some real questions about the future development of public education. Is it possible that collective negotiations may impede rather than assist the improvement of public education? Will the advent of the full-time local leader of the teacher organization have any negative effects on American education? When the local organization develops as a power center, will the full-time leader have a vested interest in conflict with the school administration and school board? Will militancy pay off for him in terms of membership support?

Will collective negotiations discourage excellence in teacher performance? In private employment collective bargaining has usually resulted in an increased emphasis on seniority and equal hours of work for all employees. Is it possible that collective negotiations will cause a standardization of teaching performance at a rather mediocre level?

Finally, and by no means the least important, will collective negotiations impede technological change in education? The next ten years will probably bring the most rapid technological change that American education has ever seen. What will the effect of a strong teacher organization be on the introduction of new teaching techniques and methods?

Regardless of the above questions, it is clear that the collective negotiations movement is here to stay, and there is no question that an increasing number of school boards will negotiate with teacher organizations in future years. The final impact, of course, will depend on how educational leaders guide the collective negotiations movement. It is my sincere hope that it will be directed in a manner that improves the education of our children.

## REFERENCES

1. National Education Association, *Addresses and Proceedings 1962*, Washington, D.C.: National Education Association, 1962, p. 178.
2. National Education Association, *NEA Handbook*, Washington, D.C.: National Education Association, 1965, p. 63.
3. Ibid. p. 65.
4. Office of Professional Development and Welfare, National Education Association, *Guidelines for Professional Negotiations*, revised edition, Washington, D.C.: National Education Association, 1965.
5. Mancur Olson, Jr., *The Logic of Collective Action*, Cambridge, Mass.: Harvard University Press, 1965.
6. From a speech presented by Dr. T. M. Stinnett at the 1966 AASA Convention in Atlantic City, New Jersey.
7. Michigan Association of Secondary School Principals, Resolutions 6-7 adopted at The Annual Convention, December 3, 1965, Grand Rapids, Michigan.

# Technology and Education

JUERGEN SCHMANDT

In the conditions of modern life the rule is absolute, the race which does not value trained intelligence is doomed. . . . Today we maintain ourselves. Tomorrow science will have moved forward yet one more step, and there will be no appeal from the judgment which will then be pronounced on the uneducated.

ALFRED NORTH WHITEHEAD (1912)

We are now at the point where we must educate people in what nobody knew yesterday and prepare in our schools for what no one knows yet, but what some people *must* know tomorrow.

MARGARET MEAD

## I. Introduction

Few would disagree that ours is a time of rapid and radical change for the educational system: for the numbers of people involved, either as teachers or as students; in the methods of training and learning that are being used; and in the role which education plays in our society. There is discussion, naturally, on *why* these changes take place and why they are taking place right *now*.

Some see more and better education for more and more people primarily as a political goal. Education, they say, produces responsible citizens, the elements of a modern democratic system. Others may think first of affluent parents' desire of academic degrees for their children, partly in search for higher social status and partly in recognition of the university's function as a gateway to rewarding careers. Still others may think of the increased technical content of education which is needed for acquiring the skills necessary for jobs in an advanced industrial economy. Over and above all this, we all believe strongly that education is a good thing in itself, that it enriches the life of the individual, that it produces a different and, we claim, a better human being; and the better man, we hope, will enable us to make progress in building a new and better society.

All these expectations, trends, and developments (and there are others I have not mentioned, such as the post World War II baby-boom) have contributed to the educational explosion of the last two decades. Any effort to explain this revolution by relating it to just one *single* cause would be an over-simplification—perhaps more misleading than helpful in an attempt to understand what is going on and in anticipating what will happen next.

I want to make this clear before turning to the question of how technology and education affect each other. Here I shall, in fact, single out one particular factor that causes change in education. To do so is a necessary step in the analysis; but as important as the impact of technology on education may be, the discussion has to be seen in the context of the wider range of problems referred to above.

Our question is this: What is the impact of technology on education? I suggest looking for an answer in three steps. We shall begin with a glance at some of the new technological devices developed for making teaching and learning easier and more efficient. We will be less interested in precisely how these machines work than in how they will change the process of education and the job of the teacher. Then we shall leave the classroom and ask: What are some of the specific demands that a technological society places on the educational system? Finally, we shall raise an even more general question about the role of education in our age. We shall make a case for understanding education as society's principal instrument for preserving itself. As such it aims at continuity and stability. How are these aims affected in a technological culture, in a culture which systematically creates change? We shall ask if there is a conflict, actual or potential, between the goal of education—stability—and the nature of technology—change?

## II. Technology for Education

The first thing that comes to mind when we talk about the new technology for education is teaching machines. They were developed in their first successful forms not much more than a decade ago.[1] Just a few years after this event, they were credited with causing "the greatest revolution in teaching methods since the invention of the printing press."[2] The event is so recent that it may be the better part of wisdom to qualify this statement by saying that the teaching machine has the potential for revolutionizing the educational system. So far the machine has not yet passed the test of large-scale usage (except perhaps in the context of specialized training, in particular, military training) and relatively few of the new devices have as yet found their way into the ordinary classroom.

But even so the new technology has grown fast. When B. F. Skinner, the Harvard psychology professor who "invented" the machine, demonstrated the new device in a meeting at the University of Pittsburgh, a faculty member asked his neighbor unbelievingly, "Is he kidding?"[3] That was in 1954. Today there is considerable argument for and against teaching machines, but everyone takes them seriously, including those who are opposed to them.

What is so new, so revolutionary about these machines? They have certain characteristics that clearly distinguish them from other technological aids for education. To understand the difference, let us recall what some of these more traditional devices are. Jerome Bruner[4] classifies them in three groups: first, devices by which the student is given "vicarious," though direct, experience of events—educational films and television, sound recordings, and the like; second, "models" (e.g., the model of the structure of the atom) which help the student grasp the underlying structure of a phenomenon and lead him step by step to the main idea; third, "dramatizing devices" which may be an historical novel about the French Revolution or a documentary on Winston Churchill or an account of Nansen's exploration of the North Pole. These aids to teaching are not new; they were used when we went to school ourselves. Today, perhaps, they are technically improved and more widely used.[5]

Let us turn now to what are at present called "teaching machines."[6] Their most outstanding feature is their capability to make the student respond to questions asked by the machine. In their more sophisticated and more expensive forms, the machines are linked to a computer, which, in turn, responds to the student's answers by indicating whether they are right or wrong. Depending on the outcome of this "dialogue," the machine then might do one of four things: (1) go on to the next problem, (2) skip ahead to more advanced materials if the student's performance is outstanding, (3) go back to part of the program that the student apparently has not yet mastered, or (4) return to an entirely different course that gives the basis for the present work.

Such programs having differential treatment for different abilities and aptitudes are called "intrinsic" or "branching" programs. They are more versatile, at least for the teaching of certain subjects, than Skinner's "linear" programs, which present the same material to all students in the same order but at least permit each individual to work at the rate which suits him best.[7] The branching program, in the words of its principal developer, N. Crowder,

represents an automation of the classical process of individual tutoring. The student is given the material to be learned in small logical units . . . and is tested on each unit immediately. The test result is used automatically to control the material that the student sees next. If the student passes the test question, he is automatically given the next unit of information and the next question. If he fails the question, the preceding unit of information is reviewed, the nature of the error is explained to him and he is retested. The questions are multiple-choice questions, and there is a separate set of correctional material for each wrong answer that is included in the multiple-choice alternatives.[8]

Both linear and branching programs, by the way, were first developed in textbook form. But printed material becomes extremely bulky and inconvenient to use. The machine can more effectively store and make available all the information needed. I say this to recall the obvious which, nevertheless, we tend to forget occasionally: that programed teaching is simply a method of presenting teaching in a carefully planned way, that the machine does not produce the program, that it simply presents it in a new way. The machine's potential to use different means of communication—pictures, sound, and written material —further differentiates it from the textbook.

Still another potential of machine teaching might become important for the teacher: he would now receive immediate information on how his students are doing, where they are having difficulties, and who needs special attention. Thus the teacher would keep in much closer and constant contact with the work of each student than was ever possible by conventional means, except for a few rich people who could pay for a private tutor for their son.

But perhaps I went too far here when I implied that there would still be someone called "teacher." Some people, in fact, have speculated that the teaching machine might displace the teacher altogether or downgrade him to a "super disc-jockey pumping out canned tuition prepared by others" or to an "educational machine-minder."[9] This fear understandably accounted for much of the initial hostility to teaching machines. Now a more balanced view seems to prevail in the discussion. It admits that certain functions in the teaching process, such as the drumming-in of facts, might be done more efficiently by machines than by people. The teacher as a drill master should be replaced by machines—by all means! Machines are also better for making visual complex mathematical or engineering problems.

But there are other aspects of the teacher's job in which he is needed as a man, as a model human being, as an experienced counselor to younger people. Bruner reminds us of Whitehead's remark that education should involve an exposure to greatness. For this we definitely need humanistic teachers, and no machine will ever be able to automate *them* out of their jobs. Bruner concludes:

> The teacher's task as communicator, model and identification figure can be supported by a wise use of a variety of devices that expand experience, clarify it, and give it personal significance. There need be no conflict between the teacher and the aids to teaching. There will be no conflict if the development of aids takes into account the aims and requirements of teaching.[10]

It may be comforting to be thus reassured that the age-old profession of the educator will still be part of tomorrow's world. There will be teachers; there will be schools; there will be students. However, these terms tomorrow may denote things radically different from what they denote today. The new technology has the potential for creating a completely different educational world. No one knows exactly how it will look and when it will come. Only time and experience will tell. But even though our image of the future can be no more than speculation —a dream, perhaps, or a nightmare—it makes sense to think about "possible futures," futures that are more likely to become reality than others.

Here is one such possible future for the world of education. In this Vision, education at all its different levels has a powerful technological aid at its disposal: a nationwide, perhaps worldwide, electronic information network which stores the world's knowledge in all fields and is accessible to the entire population. Suitable terminals, computer consoles, would be located everywhere—in schoolhouses, in offices, in homes. The development of such a system is technologically feasible, at least in principle. It might serve many interrelated purposes. But here we are interested only in the potential use of the system for education.

The system would instantly connect each student with the collection of any large library—of new videotape and film libraries, as well as traditional book libraries with instantaneous television or hard copy transmission. It would give the student access to recorded lessons on specialized topics, to teaching programs specially prepared to be understood by children of different ages, and to index systems that would lead the student to the information for which he is looking. So much on the "hardware" of the system.

So that the system can be used for large-scale educational purposes, two non-technical functions have to be fulfilled. Both "authors" and "teachers" are needed. The *authors* produce the teaching programs, a job that will require more varied skills and knowledge than were needed when we had just textbooks to work with. The new programs will be produced by teams of the best people in their respective fields: scholars, artists, teachers, experts in the processes of learning and teaching, and engineers. The model is clearly the experience gained in recent years by groups preparing new elementary and secondary school curricula which attempt to present the subject matter effectively, not only from the point of view of coverage but also of structure, in order that the child understand how things are related.[11]

This movement started under the impact of the Sputnik shock and the new concern about American scientific and technical supremacy and has spread more recently to the teaching of the social sciences and humanities. One group preparing new school curricula, led by a Nobel prize winner from the Massachusetts Institute of Technology, broke the ice and ended the long tradition of distinguished (and less distinguished) scholars looking down with little interest or even contempt on what was going on in the lowly realm of elementary and secondary school teaching.

Tomorrow's educational programs will be prepared by a new breed of educational professionalists assisted by people from all spheres of intellectual life. They will work in organizations that we do not yet have: in educational business enterprises, in non-profit organizations, or in in-house institutes of the information networks. Only early forms of the new educational enterprises are emerging now.

Hardly a week or month goes by without an announcement from some electronics manufacturer or publishing firm that it

is entering the 'education market' via merger, acquisition, joint
venture, or some other working arrangement.[12]

The production will have to be organized on a large scale.
Regional or even local productions will be sharply limited by
the high costs involved. Wide coverage, on the other hand, will
make it possible to attract the best talent for program authors.

The new *teacher* will have to be more a master of people
than of data. He will have to provide guidance and inspiration.
He will teach what questions to ask and how to ask them. He
will bring the students together for discussion groups, laboratory exercises, workshops, and study groups. This could be
easily misunderstood. The new teacher will not be like a camp
counselor, leading group activities and leaving the intellectual
part of education to the machine. He has to be able to introduce
his students to the intellectual endeavor, to its meaning and
methods, to its pains and rewards; he must make them understand what this endeavor means for our society. The need for
exposure to greatness in education, to which we referred earlier,
exists both for social and intellectual experience. In fact, any
effort to separate the two would be dangerous in a scientific
society.

The teacher would thus be freed of the most time-consuming
drilling chores of older times and would be available for educat-
ing his students as social and intellectual beings. He could do
so by keeping in close contact with each of his students
individually. The teacher might become what he was unable
to be in a mass educational system—a mentor, a Socratic guide
for each of his students.

> Indeed, guidance is all important since the individual has
> greater responsibility for his own education than he has had
> in the past; the teacher's role thus becomes far more human-
> istic and far less mechanical than it is now.

This quotation is from a research proposal by Anthony G.
Oettinger, who is the author of the Vision that I have been
talking about.[13] No one knows whether tomorrow's educational

system will be anything like Mr. Oettinger's Vision. But speculation of this kind aims less toward predicting the future with
any degree of exactness than toward giving a more concrete
frame for thinking about the social impact of possible technological developments. It is a device for raising questions, a
mechanism for counteracting the dangerous habit of starting
to think about social effects of technological innovations only
*after* they have become part of our world.

Oettinger's starting point is simply this: We have, he argues,
the technological know-how for building a nationwide electronic
information system. We also have an urgent need for coming
to terms with the problems raised by the education explosion.
Therefore, would it not be timely to ask questions like the one
previously discussed on the changing role of the teacher in an
educational system that makes full use of advances in information technology? Or to ask what the Vision would mean for
students, for schools, for parents, and for industry, universities,
and society in general? What are the promises, what are the
threats of the Vision? Will it advance or distort the purposes
of education?

What would be the reaction of the educational Establishment?
Would it accelerate or retard progress? How would the school
be organized? Would it have classes? If the student now progresses through the system as rapidly as he can or wishes to,
does there remain any intellectual need for separation of children
into grades? Would the faster individual pace with which the
student advances help in reducing the enormous waste of effort
and time and talent which we have not been able to overcome
in our present system, in which out of one hundred children
entering high school, for example, more than thirty will never
graduate? Could the Vision relieve the school of what is now the
bulk of its concern, the abstract and verbal, and permit it to concentrate on the concrete, the social, and the human?

Would the new teacher be able to broaden our traditional
view of academic excellence based almost exclusively on intellectual achievement? Could he develop in his students better
than before such significant qualities as leadership, imagination,

determination, persistence, entrepreneurial drive, and creativity? Will the system make the transition from the period of full-time schooling to the world of work easier, with the former student continuing to have access to the same information system with which he worked while he was in school? Would the Vision provide the answer to the need—so much talked about and yet so far from reality—for life-long education in a world of rapid change?

How would the system be organized? What would be the respective roles of federal, state, and local governments? What kinds of safeguards are needed to prevent abuse of the system, be it for commercial publicity or for political indoctrination? Will some sort of quality control of the programs offered be necessary? What mix between market mechanism and public control would be most desirable for the new education industry?

There are innumerable questions. They force us to see that the consequences of a nationwide electronic education network would be enormous, and that is about all we really know. We do not even know whether the beneficial aspects would out-weigh the negative side effects, or how the latter could best be minimized. There is a vast field for thinking through and testing some of the hypotheses and their possible consequences.

Mr. Oettinger, assisted by an interdisciplinary research group, has been engaged in this effort for the last two years. His main conclusion is that the promise of the Vision is light years away from the state of secondary education in America now, and, in all probability, ten or fifteen years hence.[14] His sobering findings have to do with the immaturity of educational technology and with the institutional rigidity of the American school system. A few words on each of these two principal conclusions may help in order to understand Oettinger's findings.

A close look at the current status of educational technology reveals that it is as yet much more primitive than is generally appreciated. Fragile, unreliable, and expensive devices are being developed and enthusiastically promoted. All too often this results in rapidly disenchanted customers and expensive devices which gather dust in a classroom corner. Or teachers are afraid that the complicated equipment will be damaged and try to master the problem by defining a rigid set of rules for student behavior toward machines that is reminiscent of the world of 1984. That a new technology has to go through a troublesome infancy before it is ready for large-scale use is nothing new. The critique is rather directed against the tendency, typical of much of the new educational industry and its governmental and academic supporters, to talk and write as if the development phase were completed and a combination of computers and systems analysis were standing by ready to revolutionize and modernize American education. Bridging the gap between current performance and long-term potential will need much more patient and self-critical research and development work than is now being undertaken by industry or supported by government.

The biggest obstacle, however, to the effective introduction of new technology in education is likely to be institutional. In Oettinger's words, "The educational establishment of the United States seems ideally designed to resist change." It has all the rigidity of a large bureaucracy, without much of the countervailing centralized decision-making power that ultimately makes the military or the government move. It also has the disadvantages of many small-scale organizations—fragmentation, extreme decentralization, insufficient resources—without being able to develop their points of strength—initiative, flexibility, imaginative solutions. Several case studies show how spectacularly unsuccessful attempts have been to graft the new technologies to old curricula, rigid organizations, and traditional attitudes. Oettinger concludes with a plea for introducing elements of competition and pluralism into the school system. Such institutional change, in his opinion, might lead to an environment capable of full use of the real potential of technology for education.

## III. Education for Technology

If we know as yet so little about the consequences of new educational technology for the substance and goals of education, why then should we think at all in terms of such radical changes? Why should we provoke and accelerate them by committing all the money and talent that will be needed to bring them about?

After all, we might say, our present system may have its weaknesses, but it also has impressive achievements to its credit. Where else in the world has almost universal high school enrollment been attained? Have not our schools proved to be more flexible and responsive to new demands than most critics would have thought possible? Would it not be the wisest policy to continue with what we have done in the past: to build more schools, to employ more teachers at salaries that gradually become attractive, to educate more students, and to improve the curricula? And in doing all this, we would work hard to improve the quality of American education and thus eliminate weaknesses in the system step by step. Can we not go on expanding in response to rising demands without changing the entire structure and methods of American education as they have developed historically?

This might seem to be a reasonable point of view, progressive and conservative at the same time. However, I do not think that it is a realistic point of view, partly because it underestimates the unbroken strength of man's curiosity and his drive for innovation. Sooner or later he will try new ways of doing old things, whenever science and technology give him new tools with which to experiment. One might object by saying this is a policy of change for the sake of change. Perhaps this is true, but think of the paramount role that this drive for new things—things to be discovered, to be understood, to be made by man—has played in our culture and continues to play in these days, perhaps nowhere more vigorously than in this country. Certainly this raises important and yet unsolved questions about our capability to master the world of new things that we are constantly producing in order that we do not become its slaves. We would commit social suicide, however, if our answer were to be in the direction of restricting scientific research and new technological developments.

There are, in addition, more visible and perhaps less controversial reasons which call for extensive changes in our methods and organization of education, not necessarily—to say this again—in the direction of Mr. Oettinger's Vision, but in ways which do make full use of new possibilities offered by technology. I think here of the different and higher educational requirements for the work force in an advanced industrial society. We all remember the real shock that struck this country in the aftermath of the Russian space breakthrough in 1957 and the many critical questions that were asked. Is our teaching of science and engineering outdated? Are we doing enough to attract young people to these fields? Are we running the risk of a severe shortage of qualified manpower: scientists, engineers, science teachers, Ph.D.'s, and technicians? Do we know enough about our future manpower needs, what kinds of people we shall need, and what kind of training they should receive?

Perhaps for the first time education was in the forefront of an exciting debate of nationwide scope and importance. America's political leadership, her technological supremacy, and her economic performance were at stake, and all were suddenly seen in the closest possible relationship to the American system of education. Education in general and science education in particular became a matter of high priority to the nation. Educational planning and manpower forecasting became the concern of scholars and of government officials, who were shocked to discover an almost unbelievable inadequacy of data and knowledge, without which policy was bound to be blind. Only gradually did new theories and thinking develop and find their way into action.[15]

We know about the far-reaching impact which this new concern and new thinking had on the educational enterprise. Right now we are in the middle of an unprecedented expansion of the educational system (which may begin to taper off in the early 1970's) for training the millions of young people eager to enter the work force. The projected increase of the labor force in this decade amounts to twelve and a half million people; six million of them will be under twenty-five years of age. Between 1950 and 1960 less than half a million people under twenty-five joined the labor force! The great majority of people know that

> the amount and quality of their education and training will be of particular importance both to them personally and to the nation. Competition among these 6 million extra young workers for the available jobs will be very keen. Those who have better education and training will have the advantage in this contest.[16]

These six million young people, along with a great number of older members of the work force, know that more education will mean greater income and more challenging work and may well mean the difference between being employed and being unemployed, since the proportion of jobs requiring less skills and training seems to be shrinking, and skilled white-collar and professional workers are in greater demand. The rise in educational requirements for many kinds of work is related to changes in the nature of jobs which, in turn, are related to technological change.

In this paper I do not intend to discuss in any detail the relationship between technology and changes in the nature of work.[17] Instead I should like to look briefly at the situation in other parts of the world, where tasks of equally impressive dimensions (perhaps even more impressive considering the lower level of departure) have to be accomplished in order that the educational system adjust to the needs of an advanced technological age.

The new concern about education and the realization of its close relation to economic and social progress and to political status in the world developed in Europe years later than in the United States. In many places it had to overcome considerable resistance before it could find its way into plans for action. This is not surprising in countries in which the humanistic tradition of education continues to be strong, a tradition often seen as being directly opposed to the pragmatic educational goals of a science-oriented age. Concurrently the view was strong that universities educated a numerically small elite and not all those who might personally benefit from higher education. This led to a severe underrepresentation in the universities of the workingman's children.

A decade ago in Europe, the expressions "educational planning," "economics of education," and "human capital" were largely unheard of. Or worse, they were viewed with suspicion and identified with communistic or materialistic ideology and practice. Since then, things have changed considerably. The breakthrough was to a considerable extent due to a single event, an international conference held in Washington in 1961 on "Economic Growth and Investment in Education."[18] For many Europeans, in particular for government officials and politicians, this meeting opened new horizons. Spurred by the double example of Russia and America, Europe began to move.

Today every political manifesto features more education for a larger proportion of the population as a prominent promise. Numbers of students and faculty rise steeply, as do educational budgets. More new universities are opening than ever before in the last century. But this is only a beginning, and even the most advanced countries in Europe still have a long way to go before secondary education becomes universal and higher education the common educational experience of the majority, as is the case in the United States. The disparity, indeed, is great. Out of one hundred young Americans approximately seventy will graduate from high school, but only twenty of one hundred young Europeans will attend full-time school up to the same age, or about forty in the more advanced countries in Europe. A group of European observers came to this conclusion:

> While most countries have as yet completed only the first stage of educational advance—the provision of universal elementary

education—the United States has long recognized that universal secondary education is necessary in an advanced industrial society, and has now virtually completed this second stage. In fact, it is well into a third stage in which higher education will also become universal.[19]

A word of caution should be added. The comparisons that we have mentioned seem to indicate an impressive record of American success in making advanced education a common good for the majority of the young generation. But we should not overlook the fact that these comparisons are numerical and do not take into account any qualitative differences between European and American educational systems. I am not suggesting that careful analysis of these factors would necessarily lead to significantly different results. However, until we have such a thorough comparative study, we must be careful not to overestimate the conclusiveness of merely quantitative comparisons.

In the context of this paper the few remarks about Europe were to make the point that all countries with a highly industrialized economy—we might as well call them technological societies—have to devote considerable resources to the expansion of their educational facilities in order to keep this type of economy running and growing.

This might seem to contradict the widely-held belief that automation will replace workers by machines. This is true to a considerable extent for unskilled and semi-skilled workers, but not—as presently available knowledge indicates—for white-collar work and professional and technical occupations. It is exactly these categories of people that account for a steadily increasing percentage of the total work force. The majority of the American labor force today is occupied in service functions. Such an occupational structure is unique in the world, and has never existed before. The close relationship between unemployment, or the danger of unemployment, and low levels of education was pointed out prominently in the 1966 report of the President's Automation Commission. The report concludes:

Unemployment tends to be concentrated among those workers with little education, not primarily because technological developments are changing the nature of jobs, but because the uneducated are at the 'back of the line' in competition for jobs. Education, in part, determines the employability and productivity of the individual, the adaptability of the labor force, the growth and vitality of the economy, and the quality of the society.[20]

In other words, a higher level of education—general education, not vocational training in particular skills—determines people's status, income, and employability in the labor force. The specific skills demanded from any given individual may change significantly during his working life, and he must have enough education to be able to learn new things as they are needed for keeping him employed.

## IV. Change Versus Stability

We have talked about the new technology for education, the opportunities it offers for making education more efficient and more widespread and for freeing the teacher for his real job—preparing young people for becoming citizens of a world in which change is the new reality. We then talked about the massive educational requirements of a technology-based economy.

Both themes clearly need to be seen together. One, the demand for more education for more people, might be called the challenge; the other, expanding and improving education by technological means, the response, to use Arnold Toynbee's categories. The response, we said, can take different forms, but all of them will have to rely heavily on the assistance provided by technology. The one alternative which we do not have, I tried to suggest, is that of doing the job that needs doing by just using the old methods. This, at least in the long run, would be a self-defeating policy. The task ahead is so big that using the old methods alone would require our becoming a nation of nothing but teachers and students. Other social functions would suffer from such an overcommitment of scarce resources

to just one function—education. Our goals of education, maximum and improved education for a maximum number of
people, are only attainable to the extent that we are prepared
to look for new ways for doing the job. And we are used to
looking toward science and technology to provide us with the
new tools we need.

The same argument could be made for a somewhat different
reason. I have been talking about the need for a radical reform
of the educational system. But is it at all realistic to aim toward
radically changing a strong, tradition-honored system? Would
not whoever tried risk immediate burial beneath the uproar of
resistance that would surround him from both inside and outside the Establishment? R. Buckminster Fuller, one of the few
provocative and thoughtful speculators of our times, suggests
a "technological fix" answer to this question: changing the
system of American education by administrative, political decision would be quite hopeless an undertaking. But many of the
obstacles to change might disappear, since they would become
obsolete, if the system were changed from inside by introducing
what he calls new "design competence," a new technological
system that, once introduced, would automatically call for a
complete overhaul of the educational system in all its ramifications.[21] In other words, technology bought as a gadget by the
customer might be powerful enough to break up organizational
and behavioral patterns that have become too rigid.

This leads to one last question: Is there tension or conflict,
actual or potential, between education and technology, a conflict which originates in their different relations to stability and
change? Education transmits and preserves what exists, whereas
innovation and discovery are the essence of technology and
science. What is the role of education in a world which deliberately develops science and technology as vehicles of social
change?

Philosophers like Hegel and Dewey have emphasized the
stabilizing function of education, education as a life experience,
not just as a formal process that we go through in our youth.
Education, they say, is like a second birth; it gives man his

social and cultural existence. Education is the privilege of man; animals may be trained, never educated. It gives man access to the richness of former worlds and makes him into an historical being. Education is the way by which societies keep alive and pass on their knowledge and institutions to the next generation. Education, in short, preserves society.

Biologists like Portmann came to similar views about the social role of education, though for different reasons. Compared with a newborn animal, Portmann pointed out, the human baby is born prematurely—helpless, unfinished, and unprotected. *Physiologically* man is an underdeveloped animal. He does not reach a stage of physiological development comparable to that of the animal at its moment of birth until a year after this event. But this first year of the human life span—and this is the significant point—is spent from the very first day in a social environment in which the child, even though his own parents may not yet notice this, is learning, is in communication with others. He is weak, but open to learning.

Education is viewed here as creating man as a social being and as preserving the world in which man lives—society. Such an interpretation helps us understand why it makes good sense to say that education aims at creating stability. It makes sense both for the individual and for society. But stability is not the same as immobility. Man builds the world in which he lives himself. The stability which he builds for his protection and guidance—habits, traditions, laws, institutions, etc.—is not of the absolute nature of, say, animal instincts. Man is capable of changing man-made stability. To make people see that the stability around them or the apparent loss of it is their own work, that it can be controlled and influenced at will, that there can be change in stability, that change can occur without making life unstable to the extent that it would be unbearable and would dissolve society—these are perhaps the most difficult tasks of the educator in an age that is changing as other ages have but is different from them because change is no longer just happening but is being deliberately created as the motor of progress.

In some way we all prefer habit to innovation, stability to change. Or we might say, we like change to the extent that we can see where it leads, but we instinctively resist change that would overwhelm us. The degree of what is considered as being acceptable change clearly differs with time. For the nineteenth-century farmer or workingman, the yearly vacation trip to a distant part of the country, to take a very simple example, would have been a frightening idea, even long after the advent of railroads. Today vacation mobility is part of the habit pattern of almost all segments of the population. Tomorrow job mobility may become equally natural and be viewed as a challenge rather than a plight.

If education, as the Vision would suggest, becomes a permanent part of our lives, not just the occupation of a few years spent at school, then clearly people would be better educated to live with change without being overcome by it. The information and education system itself would be an element of stability (comparable somewhat to the educational function of the Bible in former times) because it would accompany man through all his life. The system, devised by technology, would help people to see that what remains stable behind radical and constant change are the methods of doing things and the ways for approaching problems.[22]

## REFERENCES

1. A good historical account, beginning with early but soon forgotten work by S. Pressey in 1926, is to be found in W. Kenneth Richmond, *Teachers and Machines, An Introduction to the Theory and Practice of Programmed Learning*, London: Collins, 1965.
2. "The New Educational Technology," a speech issue of *The American Behavioral Scientist*, November 1962, p. 9.
3. Ibid. p. 56.
4. Chapter entitled "Aids to Teaching," Jerome Bruner, *The Process of Education*, New York: Vintage Books, 1960.
5. See for a review of some more recent developments "Technology of Education," a special issue of *Discovery* (England), Decem-

ber 1965, in particular the article by N. E. Willis, "Teacher or Technician?"

6. Incidentally, some of the opposition to them may be simply linguistic. It would be nice indeed if someone would come up with a simpler and less mechanistic term. History gives us some hope for this to happen. We know of other examples of crude names given to new inventions during their infancy, such as the aerostatic machine, which was the first name given to the balloon.

7. See Richmond, *Teachers and Machines*, pp. 44-54.

8. N. Crowder, "Automatic Tutoring by Means of Intrinsic Programming," in E. Galanter, ed., *Automatic Teaching: The State of the Art*, New York: Wiley, 1959.

9. "Technology of Education," *Discovery*, December 1965, p. 28.

10. Bruner, "Aids to Teaching," p. 91.

11. Ibid. pp. 6-12. See also Jerome B. Wiesner, "Innovation and Experimentation in Education," *Science and Society: A Symposium*, Xerox Corporation, 1965.

12. Harold Howe II, then United States Commissioner of Education, in an address before the American Management Association's First Practicum in Educational Technology, New York: August 9, 1966.

13. See Anthony G. Oettinger, "A Vision of Technology and Education," *Communications of the ACM*, July 1966, p. 3. Reprinted as No. 1 of the Reprint Series of the Harvard University Program on Technology and Society.

14. See Anthony G. Oettinger with the collaboration of Sema Marks, *Run, Computer, Run: The Mythology of Educational Innovation*, Cambridge, Mass.: Harvard University Press, Spring 1969; Anthony Oettinger and Sema Marks, "Educational Technology: New Myths and Old Realities," and a "Reply" to six critics, *Harvard Educational Review*, Vol. 38, No. 4 (Fall 1968), pp. 697-717, 751-755. Reprinted as No. 6 of the Reprint Series of the Program on Technology and Society.

15. The literature in such areas as "economics of education" and "forecasting of manpower needs" has grown rapidly. The following are a few representative publications:
Seymour Harris, *The Economics of Higher Education in the United States*, New York: McGraw-Hill, 1962;
Frederick Harbison and Charles Myers, *Education, Manpower and Economic Growth*, New York: McGraw-Hill, 1964;

Garth L. Mangum, ed., *The Manpower Revolution: Its Policy Consequences*, excerpts from Senate Hearings before the Clark Subcommittee, Garden City, N.Y.: Doubleday, 1965;

OECD, Study Group in the Economics of Education, *The Residual Factor and Economic Growth*, Paris: 1964;

Jon T. Innes *et al., The Economic Returns to Education*, A Survey of the Findings, Center for the Advanced Study of Educational Administration, Eugene, Oregon: 1965.

16. Harold Goldstein, then Assistant Commissioner for Manpower and Employment Statistics, in Hearings before the Senate Committee on Labor and Public Welfare, 1963. Quoted in Mangum, ed., *The Manpower Revolution*, p. 14.

17. See for a summary of the debate and literature, Harvard University, Program on Technology and Society, Research Review No. 2, *Technology and Work*, Cambridge: Winter 1969.

18. OECD, *Policy Conference on Economic Growth and Investment in Education*, 5 volumes, Paris, 1962.

19. OECD, *Higher Education and the Demand for Scientific Manpower in the United States*, Paris, 1963, p. 63.

20. Report of the National Commission on Technology, Automation and Economic Progress, *Technology and the American Economy*, Vol. 1, February 1966, p. 110. Six volumes of preparatory studies were published as separate appendices. Volume 4 of these is entitled *Educational Implications of Technological Change*.

21. R. Buckminster Fuller, *Education Automation, Freeing the Scholar to Return to His Studies*, Carbondale, Ill.: Southern Illinois University Press, 1962, p. 16.

22. See E. G. Mesthene, "Learning To Live with Science," *Saturday Review*, July 17, 1965.

# Humanistic Approaches to the
# Design of Schools

## JOHN F. COGSWELL

Ever since Sputnik threatened our national image, there has been a clamoring to turn to the ingenuity of our industrial and scientific complex, to computer-type systems, to improve our schools. But the tendency to equate machines and people as resources may have dangerous consequences; the desire for control and efficiency attracts the researcher to the machine and tends to ignore the human teacher and the attitudes, feelings, and inclinations of the student. We should not expect that we can find ultimate answers. But if the word "humanistic" is to have real meaning in our work with the schools, procedures must be developed that put and keep the human being central in the system.

The purpose of this paper is twofold. First of all, I want to clarify my concern about the human problem in the design and development of schools. And secondly, I want to describe some recent attempts that we at System Development Corporation have been making in our work in education to find humanistic approaches to the development of schools. I will discuss particularly our work in the design of a man-machine counseling system and our work in the study of school organization by means of computer simulation.

I think I can fairly well sum up the major objectives that guided this work until recently. We were interested in (1) viewing schools as man-machine systems that could be developed by the same system procedures that were used to develop systems in other areas, such as military systems, and (2) finding ways that the new information processing or computer technology could be applied to education.

During the same time period that I have been involved in

educational research, I also have been working intensively with persons in individual and group psychotherapy. As time has gone along, I have become aware of a grating dissonance between my experience in educational research and my experience doing psychotherapy. Although both of these activities seemed to be oriented toward helping people—in one case indirectly by improving education, and in the other case by direct encounter with people—I found that in my private practice I was using my energies trying to help people to become less like machines and more like human beings, while, in my educational research, I developed the growing fear that I might be helping people to become more and more like machines.

It is clear that many people are coming for psychotherapy because they are trying to treat themselves in a cold way like machines that can be beaten and coerced into higher production by pushing themselves to achieve, to be efficient, and to ignore their feelings. Their desires for human contact, for physical and emotional comfort, and their needs to love and care for themselves are seen as threats to their attempts to make themselves efficient and productive like machines. So, through ever-increasing efforts, they deny these kinds of human feelings and are intolerant of themselves for ever having had them. It needs to be clear that I am not talking about raving maniacs, but about intelligent professional people who are functioning in society—people who come to therapy to try to find themselves and who want to actualize themselves and live their lives fully. When they finally do become aware of their feelings, they also frequently become aware of tremendous hurting and sadness in themselves that has accumulated from their self-hatred and intolerance. My job as a therapist is to help them to trust and respect their feelings and to increase their awareness of the struggle to live their own lives. When they become aware of and accept their caring for themselves, they are no longer able to treat themselves and others with indifference. They sometimes change their fields of work so that they spend their lives doing what is really gratifying to them, even though they may have spent twenty years or more in a field in which, although

they were successful, they were not happy. They become aware
of their caring for others and are able to develop deep relationships with others and a genuine caring for and identification
with humanity.

My work in education, on the other hand, seemed, until
recently, to have been focused in a different direction. I found
that by using the traditional systems approach I was tending
to look at schools as if they were production machines. The
system development model used with military weapons systems
or with industry rests on several assumptions. One of these
is that a system, such as our Air Defense System, exists for the
purpose of achieving limited but easily defined objectives. In
the case of the Air Defense System, the major objective is to
keep an accurate and timely awareness of the content of the
air environment, to detect and identify rapidly unknown objects
as they occur in the environment, and to destroy quickly any
hostile objects. These objectives are defined by the top-ranking
officers and civilians who are responsible for the system. The
basic objectives are set and tend to remain the same throughout
the life cycle of the system—from the beginning design, throughout the development phase, and for the rest of the life of the
system.

The assumption that a system exists for the purpose of
achieving limited but easily defined objectives seems to have been
valid for the development of military systems. Experience with
the application of the systems approach to the development of
large-scale military systems has demonstrated the utility of
these procedures. In fact, it was the apparent success of these
procedures in the military environment that led us to explore
their application to education.

But if these assumptions are applied to education, it requires
that authorities such as the school board and school administration define the objectives of the school. It implies that
students graduating from the system be viewed as the *output*
of the system, and all that is required is that the authorities
state what characteristics the output—the graduating students—
should have. It is assumed not only that the authorities are the

ones who should define the objectives, but also that these objectives are fairly static—that they will remain the same over a long period of time. These assumptions frighten me. Although I believe that the school does exist to meet society's needs, it is dangerous to assume that the students and teachers are not *part* of that society. To make students and faculty subject to the objectives defined by authority *and* to make them *live* constrained by these definitions over a long period of time must contribute to their sense of alienation. If they have little or no responsibility for setting their own goals, they will come to feel less and less responsible for their own lives. I fear that the very foundations of democracy are threatened by this assumption that the authority rests only with the administration.

You may answer this threat by arguing that educators will certainly resist this approach—that their interest in the needs of their students will naturally make them resist it. My experience leads me to a different conclusion. For example, we have been visited by school board members who wanted us to work with them and use this approach. Ever since Sputnik threatened our national image, there has been a clamoring to improve our educational system, on the assumption that we could turn to the ingenuity of our industrial and scientific complex for a solution. This point of view reached a high point when the Job Corps training programs were being planned. The attitude of the governmental planners of these systems was that the educational community had failed and that, if success was to be achieved, the educators should be by-passed. They turned directly to the industrial community.

I believe that we have become so immersed in viewing our educational systems as production systems we are blind to what the effects might be. Is the current hippie movement a reaction to this educational system that we are now developing? Is it a reflection of human beings struggling not to be treated as machines? Are the hippies trying to say, "I will not be a tool of society and give up what I care about," "I will not give up my awareness of life, of being a feeling, changing human being"?

Another assumption of the systems approach as it has been applied to the military is that once the system's objectives have been defined, the system can be designed and developed by technologists or system experts. Again, alienation is encouraged. The responsibility for defining the operations of the system is turned over to experts. The people who will live in and use the system tend to be treated as passive objects, to be manipulated by authority or its agents. The system planners make the assumption that men and machines can be viewed as resources and that the goal is to design a system where men and machines can be allocated to function in such a way that the system objectives can most efficiently be met.

Even if we assume that the objectives of the system could be defined really to meet the needs of the people who will live in the system, the tendency to equate machines and people as resources may have dangerous consequences. Machines are much easier to control than human beings. From the efficient designer's point of view, people may be viewed as "messy"— not easily controlled. Hence, the designer may focus most of his energies on developing the machine to perform important functions, relegating the human to fairly simple uncreative jobs. In some military systems that have been developed, men spend boring hours sitting watching displays that have been generated by the computer on cathode ray tubes, looking for errors in the computer's performance and making corrections when they are required. I think the same tendency to focus on that which seems easiest to control can be seen in the research on teaching machines.

Educational researchers talk about such things as using the machine to free the teacher to do more creative things, or developing systems where the teacher and the machine will be part of the system. But in actual fact, very few research studies have been done that pay any attention to the teacher's role. In one such study, the teacher was assigned to the role of monitoring the teaching machine. I think that this desire for control and efficiency attracts the researcher to the machine and causes him to ignore the human teacher. The researcher may even feel annoyed and hostile toward the teacher because he cannot control the teacher completely, as he can a machine.

The desire to move toward that which seems easiest to control is not limited to the selection and design of resources for education. The tendency is apparent on all levels of activity. When one operates on the assumption that the objectives of the system can be defined in behavioral or operational terms, this tendency to oversimplify becomes manifest. I suspect that the very assumption that the objectives of education can be defined operationally reflects a strong human need to seek security and safety by oversimplification. Regardless of what needs underlie such definition, it is immediately apparent that such attempts to define objectives usually focus on those behaviors that are easiest to define. The tendency is to define objectives that focus on the acquisition of facts and concepts. The attitudes, feelings, and inclinations of the student tend to be ignored when objectives are defined.

It is this struggle for security or safety through control and oversimplification that is at the heart of my concern. As I see it, American education is presently involved in an existential crisis. In its responses to the pressure of changing world and national events, it is caught in a real struggle between trying to hold onto those things in its history that have given it security and trying to be open to the here and now.

I do not believe that we can borrow directly the procedures used to develop our military and industrial complexes to develop schools in the same manner that we develop weapon systems; if we do, we may produce human beings who are more like weapons or automata than people. They may be capable of passively obeying commands, going directly to their pre-programed destinations, and blowing up other human beings with little or no feeling. One need only remember the kamikaze of World War II to realize that such an outcome is possible. Or, they may break down in the system. In fact, some of the disavowal of social responsibility seen in the hippie and psychedelic movements may be a reflection of this reaction.

I believe that more than ever before in our history we are

in need of finding ways that can allow American education to become alive and creative. We need humanistic procedures for developing our schools. But what might these procedures be? What do we mean by "humanistic"? It is difficult to define in meaningful terms the humanistic concept. Certainly, central to the idea is the notion that procedures will be developed that make the human being central in the system. It is not enough to say that schools are, in and of themselves, humanistic institutions designed for the purpose of providing education and acculturation to the students. It is not enough to say that obviously we care about people and students. It is too easy to say that we all are primarily concerned with the growth of the student and let it go at that. If the word "humanistic" is to have real meaning in our work with schools, we must find actual procedures that do, in fact, put persons into the center of this design and development process. This is not an easy goal to achieve. Certainly, from the point of view of efficiency, it seems, in a way, easier to turn over the design and development process to the so-called "system expert" or the "technologist." One can argue that, once the systems experts have obtained a clear statement of the objectives, the job of design and development can proceed most effectively without continual involvement with the persons who will use and benefit by the system. But this point is extremely important because it is at this choice point that we can develop either "open" or "closed" systems. To the extent that the persons who live in and use this system participate continuously in the never-ending design and development process, the system is open; to the extent that they are not participating in the process, the system is closed.

Another way of looking at this problem of humanistic design and development of schools is from the existential philosophical point of view. From this view we can think of the school as an organism living in a complex, changing environment. The school, like a human being, has limited control over its environment. All of the efforts and energies applied to maintaining the existence and survival of the system can be entirely futile in the event of atomic holocaust, earthquake, or tornado. Certainly, in the case of a school, the flow of funds from the community, and from the state and the Federal government, are variables over which the school has only a limited control, and yet this flow of funds has an effect upon the vitality of the school. But if the school, like the individual, is to survive, it must make choices, even though it does not have ultimate control over the consequences of its actions. If choices are made, there is some risk of failure. On the other hand, decisions may be made that enhance vitality and growth. It is extremely difficult for the individuals, and I suspect for organizations, to accept the responsibility for decisions when the consequences are so difficult to predict. Organizations probably have ways of trying to avoid awareness of their responsibility and the uncertainty of existence. Again, schools may become rigid and adhere strictly to rules and regulations and procedures, hoping that somehow by sticking strictly to the rules they will feel safe and belie the uncertainty of existence. Or, like individuals, the schools may be tempted to turn their fate and responsibility over to others— like the individual may turn to some outside authority wanting this person to take responsibility for him. To the extent that a person, an organization, or a school loses awareness of the uncertainty of existence and loses the responsibility for choice and its consequences, the entity tends to give up its viability and to relinquish what control is possible in a limited, somewhat unpredictable environment.

It is then from this existential point of view that system design and development procedures must be viewed. Those procedures that encourage the school to give up its own sense of responsibility to experts who will "give answers" tend to destroy the viability of the school. Those procedures that promise certain control over the learning process or the growth process again encourage an unreal dependency. On the other hand, those procedures that acknowledge and value the resistance of school personnel to turn over control of their classrooms to technology should be viewed as healthy.

These resistances should be viewed as signs of strength that should be encouraged rather than discouraged. It should also be recognized that there are no easy answers or pat solutions to education; a human being, to stay alive and open to his environment, must struggle to resist the temptation of defenses that promise fantasied certainty and complete control. So must the school. The design and development procedures used should be those that help the people in the school (the staff, students, parents, etc.) to be aware of themselves and their environment, to be sensitive to changes in themselves and the environment, to be aware of their choices and their responsibility for their choices, and to be willing to make behavioral commitments along with their choices.

In the remainder of this paper I want to discuss some recent struggles that we and others have been making to find humanistic procedures for the system development of schools. First, I want to talk about some studies that are aimed at trying to *involve* the people who will use the system in the design process; next, I will discuss some techniques that may have potential for expanding creative awareness in the design process; and finally, I will discuss some possible organizational characteristics for humanistically designed schools of the future.

Currently, we are trying to develop a man-machine counseling system for schools. Although our original orientation was to develop the system in accordance with the military model of system development, we have come more and more to see our objectives as twofold: (1) to develop humanistic procedures for system development; and (2) to develop designs for a counseling system that are humanistic. This project, supported by the U.S. Office of Education, is viewed as a three to four year study involving three phases—design, development, and evaluation. We are just completing the initial phase—design.

We have been working with ten counselors who comprise the staff of a large Los Angeles high school and five counselors who comprise the counseling staff of a large junior high school. We first conducted a system analysis of the counseling operations of the two schools by interviewing each of the counselors and obtaining detailed descriptions of how each of them conducted their job. We made up display charts illustrating what we thought we had learned from them. In a group meeting with the counselors we reviewed our perceptions by going over the displays, and in this way we and the counselors began to communicate more openly about the counseling operation.

Following the system analysis, we provided the counselors with a short training program on the potentials and limitations of the computer. Because we wanted them to be involved in the design process, it was necessary that they understand how the computer might be used. We were somewhat anxious before the actual design meetings were to begin. Although we believed that the counselors would come up with as many ideas as the research team, if given the chance, there was fear that the counselors would tend to defer to the research team in planning the use of the computer and that some of the researchers would take the bait by telling the counselors how to use the computer. I was also afraid that the counselors who had some experience with data processing and who liked working with data processing might dominate in the design meetings. On the other hand, I felt that the counselors who were most interested in students and least interested in data would tend to be passively resistant in the meetings. For these reasons we decided to try out the idea of using an outside person skilled in group techniques to facilitate communication during the design meetings. Dr. Gerard Haigh, representing the National Training Laboratories, offered to serve. He had a difficult role to fill. He had to facilitate communication and creativity in the group while the counselors and researchers worked together in designing the man-machine system. At the same time he had to avoid concentrating on interpersonal conflicts to the degree that the group would be diverted away from the design task toward a psychotherapy experience. We worked for twenty hours with the high school counselors, with the last twelve hours a "marathon" session from seven in the morning until seven at night. We were so involved that we worked on the design throughout the whole day.

It was the strong feeling of the research team that this use of a communication facilitator was extremely valuable. All of the counselors participated in the design process, and a strong group feeling brought the researchers and counselors into one real design group. This sense of group identity has persisted until the present, and the counselors have become much more open and involved with each other in their school counseling as a result of the experience.

Although we strongly recommend this procedure as one that does facilitate humanistic goals in the design process, it must be emphasized that these procedures cannot be instituted without a struggle. Nor can it be assumed that all people will go along with it. Although the high school counselors agreed to try the idea of using the communication facilitator, the junior high school people refused to try the idea. The head counselor perceived the idea as manipulative. Our experience with these two different reactions points to the fact that the humanistic approach does allow people to resist change and to be given free choice. We must give up the assumption that we can have complete control.

A number of design ideas did emerge from the design workshops. Since it is not the purpose of this paper to discuss this project in detail, I shall mention them briefly. They are as follows:

Storage of all student data in the computer for ready processing and retrieval.

Tracking and monitoring of student progress to alert counselors to possible problems.

On-line generation and application of multiple regression formulas for predictive and research analysis.

Automated generation of all routine reports such as grade reports and progress reports.

Automated interviews to help students in the areas of post-high-school planning, course programing, and vocational exploration.

An English-like user-language that allows each counselor to communicate with the computer in terms of his own choice of words, statements, and formats.

Although these computer systems are being developed, there was a point following the design meetings where program development almost came to a halt. As the research team became aware of what had happened, it realized that almost all of the design ideas had been for the computer. Very few creative ideas had been suggested for how the counselors would use the time that the computer would make available. The more we thought about this problem, the more we feared that the introduction of the computer into the system would result in the counselors' getting more caught up in data. We feared that, with the computer in the system, they might spend even less time in human relationships with students.

We found that, despite our efforts to work toward the design of a system for counseling that involved machines *and humans,* the total system was getting to look more like a machine than a human being. Again, despite our efforts, we found the tendency to focus on the machine rather than the human beings was very strong.

After we realized what had happened, we went back to the counselors and told them that we were disturbed. We suggested the idea of a training program in group counseling techniques. We told them that we felt that if they were more comfortable in working with students in a counseling relationship, they might use the computer to gain more free time with students. Again, the high school counselors agreed to go along with the idea. They agreed to devote two hours a week to a training program and even suggested a person in the school district who had experience in training counselors in group counseling. For the past semester they have been in the training program. They are extremely enthusiastic about their involvement with group counseling.

On the other hand, the junior high school counselors did not go along with the idea of training in group counseling. Their point of view was that counseling entails educational and vocational aspects, not personal ones, and that the sessions would not help them.

In another attempt to make the man-machine counseling system more humanistic, we worked with students and a teacher in a graduate course at UCLA in moral and ethical issues in counseling. We presented the design ideas for the man-machine system to the students and discussed the system and related issues with them. A large part of the discussion was focused on their values and the choices they would make if they were working in a school where a man-machine counseling system was being developed. The students wrote term papers that dealt with their personal ethical analysis of the system. We had two objectives for teaching the course. One objective was to expose students in counseling to the potential developments they would probably have to deal with in their work as counselors. A quote from one student's paper may give you some feeling for the reaction to the learning experience:

> After reviewing the rapid progress that is being made everywhere by the computer and data processing, it is truly amazing that so few people know anything about computers and their capabilities.
>
> A whole classroom of graduate students admitted that they knew nothing about computers, had never seen one, and could neither describe one nor explain them mechanically. They expressed indifference, confusion, discomfort, and some expressed in nonverbal ways an unwillingness to learn about the computers. The apparent discomfort grew worse when the class was asked whether or not a machine could have a value system. While some were ready to consider the problem and were ready to admit that it could have such a system, most were reluctant to say what kind of value system it should have, whose value system shou!d be used, or to consider their own value systems as suitable for programming. The subject of personal ethics was treated in a similar manner. Some claimed an invasion of privacy. There was an anguished cry from one that set the tenor of the group: 'Exploitation.'
>
> Now students who had merely been apathetic tuned in. Was there something to be inferred about future concepts of counseling? Students and professors broke for a coffee break more than slightly affected by the undercurrents. There was going to be more to this class than mere reading and parroting. More than mere surface discussion of a computer would be dealt with. We were to find a completely new world, just a few miles away.

The other objective was to try to increase our sensitivity to human ethical values in the development of the system. We have compiled the students' papers, and in the fall we will share them with the counselors. They contain many ideas that we had not thought of, and we plan to involve the students at the schools in a similar evaluation in an attempt to get an outside point of view as one means of expanding the awareness of the research team and the counselors.

Another project that is just beginning in Southern California is using some stimulating, humanistic ideas for system development. I feel that this project may be the most significant of the current American education scene. In this project, a total school system will be involved in a series of confrontation, or basic-encounter, groups. An attempt will be made to involve students, teachers, and administrators in ongoing confrontation. Teachers in some of the elementary schools and one of the high schools will meet in confrontation groups with trained facilitators where they will discuss their personal philosophies, their feelings about education, and the possibility of innovation. Following their group meetings, they will go on a traveling seminar where they will be exposed to the ideas and innovations in which others are involved. Following this exposure they will return and plan for innovation in their own schools through the medium of confrontation group meetings.

One idea in this project that I feel is especially important is the idea of the traveling seminar. As I work in the field of educational design, I am becoming increasingly impressed by the extent to which our thinking and our values are limited and determined by our experience. This may sound like an obvious truism, but I believe that it is an unconscious process: we are not aware of the extent to which we unconsciously adjust our values to fit our concrete experience.

Two different observations have led me to be concerned about this hypothesis. One of these observations was made in the man-machine counseling study mentioned above, in which an attitude inventory that we developed was adminstered to the counselors working in the high school and those who were counselors in training at UCLA. Both the school counselors and the trainees responded to the items in a way that indicated they agreed on their picture of what activities a counselor performs. But the school counselors showed a tendency to value more highly those activities in which they were engaged most of the time, while the trainees tended to value more highly those things that corresponded to their theoretical training. One interpretation of these data is that the counselors tend to adjust their values to fit what they must do. They came to see the routine processing of student data as a good. If this interpretation is valid, our fear that the counselors would use the computer to get more caught up in data has some basis.

The other observation relates to my work in the study of school organization through computer simulation. Over a two-and-one-half year period, we made intensive studies of secondary schools that were trying various forms of innovation. Three of the schools that we studied were trying to individualize instruction by employing various versions of the Continuous Progress Plan. The basic notion of this plan is that students will work on an individual basis much of the time with materials designed for individual study. They will be free to progress at their own rate. They will request help from the teacher when they need it; otherwise they will continue to work individually without interruption. When they are ready to take a test, they request it, take it, and, if they pass, continue on to the next unit. They may be brought into small-group and occasional large-group meetings for lectures, discussion, or lab work.

After studying the attempts of several schools to implement these plans, we concluded: ". . . that there is really no existing course that is completely individualized as far as the time variation dimension is concerned. Educators need to become much more sensitive to the fact that their experience in group-centered education will make it difficult for them to develop an educational system that is truly individual-centered." What led us to this conclusion was that we repeatedly found that educators who were trying to develop individualized plans were making decisions that were valid for working with students in groups, but were not valid for working with individuals.

The most outstanding example of this was our study of a tenth-grade biology course set up for individual progress. We collected data on the variations in individual progress of the students in their course work and used these data in the computer simulation modeling program that we had developed (called EDSIM) to predict how the students would distribute themselves through time as the course progressed. The assumption underlying the generation of the simulated data was that a student's rate of performance would tend to remain the same throughout the course and that the time spent in each unit of the course would be a function of the length of the unit and the student's rate of work.

When the simulated data produced by the computer were compared to the actual performance of the students in the course, a strange discrepancy was found. The rates of progress of the students varied from unit to unit. The explanation that we discovered was that the teacher was setting group deadlines for the course. The students were all being encouraged to finish a defined number of units by certain deadlines—such as the middle of the semester, the end of the first semester, and the end of the course. As a result, students would start out slowly and then speed up their rate as they approached the deadline. One student started the second semester by spending fifty days in Unit 6 and twenty-four days in Unit 7. He then completed Units 8, 9, and 10 in a total of eleven days. These findings support the contention that it is difficult for those experienced in group-centered education to develop an education system that is individual-centered.

What is needed are techniques or procedures that can help people to see alternatives and possible consequences of choices that go beyond their present experience. Certainly the idea of the traveling seminar is one fairly obvious way that awareness of potential can be increased. SDC's study of this technique does show that the educators who participated in the tour were stimulated to initiate innovations in their own schools.

The computer simulation capability (EDSIM) mentioned earlier may be another means of expanding awareness of potential. EDSIM is planned so that a designer can build a model of a school organization by specifying a population of students, the students' characteristics, the course in the school, the sequence of activities within the course, and alternative paths that a student may take within the course. The computer will "run the model," to record what would happen to the simulated students if they went through the course and followed various pathways. Alternative pathways might include the decision to continue the student in individual study, to send him to the teacher for help, or send him for testing. The decision as to whether a particular student should be branched at a certain point may be based on probability statements or on actual simulated characteristics of the students. Almost any kind of plan can be simulated by varying the specification of the students and the rules for the course.

I tried to use the EDSIM capability to explore what might happen if students in a Continuous Progress Plan course were allowed to schedule themselves autonomously. I was interested in trying to determine if I could get a feeling for the kinds of resources, such as teachers and space, that would be needed if students could do the following:

1. Work on any course they wanted to, when they wanted to, and as long as they wanted to.
2. Get help on an individual basis on the same day that it was needed.
3. Take a test on the same day that it was needed.

By simulating this extreme plan I got some feeling from the data of how a school should be organized to facilitate autonomy in student behavior. Although further exploration of the plan might lead to the discovery of loopholes that I overlooked, the data did suggest that such a plan might be feasible. Analysis of the data suggested the need for placing individual study carrels, testing stations, laboratories, and group practice rooms around the teacher. The data also suggested that students could receive individual help and tutoring with minimal delay when it would be needed.

Although I by no means view these findings as definitive, I

do feel that computer modeling techniques can be developed which will enhance people's capacity to think about some of the possible consequences of complex organizational plans. I would like to see the EDSIM capability developed so that educators involved in educational design could use it to build models, without having to know computer programing. Work at SDC was started in this direction but has been postponed for the time being because of the pressure of other projects.

To summarize, I have tried to focus on what I feel are some of the most critical issues in educational development today. As I see it, American education is in an existential crisis. We are faced with the choice of reacting to threat by turning to the fantasy that we can develop schools in the same way that we develop weapons systems or of struggling to find ways that are humanistically oriented. If we do struggle to develop open systems for human beings, the course is not an easy one. We will continually be faced with the tendency to over-simplify and the temptation to obtain a high measure of control over the process. We cannot separate the kind of school organization that we would like to have from the procedures that are used to develop the plan. No plan for school organization can be made that will meet the needs of all people for all times. We should not expect that we can find ultimate answers. Our focus should be on finding ways of involving the human beings who will live in and use the system in the development process. We should find procedures that open the school to change, and we should find procedures for keeping people involved in this change process. For years we have been faced with a constantly recurring phenomenon in education. And yet, we have failed to recognize its significance. The phenomenon is this: school morale and school performance always seem to increase when the people become involved in new experimental programs. But when the initial experimental and development phase is over, enthusiasm and performance drop even though the innovation that was tried may be maintained on an ongoing basis. We have failed to recognize that it is not the innovation alone that causes the change. We need in addition to keep the involvement in the change process as a continuing thing.

I have tried to illustrate several attempts to find ways to involve people in the development process. These are only beginnings. I have also tried to illustrate the difficulty of taking this path. But no matter how frustrating or difficult, I think the consequences of not making the choice to seek humanistic ways for school development may be devastating.

Finally, I'd like to make a few guesses as to what some of the characteristics of schools of the future might be if we follow humanistic procedures of system development. I think that spaces will be wide open. Rather than a conglomeration of boxes upon boxes of classrooms, the school will consist of large carpeted areas where numerous activities can take place at once and where change and flow of activity can take place easily. Some of our non-graded elementary schools are experimenting very successfully with these kinds of space. Three teachers, responsible for three classes of students, may share the same large space. The carpet reduces extraneous noise to the point that the students and teachers are relaxed and not overly concerned with the control of routine. Communications and flow of activity occur easily in this environment. Students and teachers will participate in planning their experiences through group discussions and in private consultation. The concept of grades or classes will eventually disappear. Students will pursue their work in both individual and group modes. The focus of the curriculum will be experiential rather than primarily abstract. Students will have an opportunity to have concrete experiences in the community as part of their education. They will have chances to synthesize and crystallize their experience in group discussion with others who have had similar experience. This opening of space and openness to the community will take place at all levels of education, and education will become a continuing activity throughout life.

The focus on learning will not be efficiency and rapid rate of performance in fixed sequences of verbal material. It will be understood that when a person wants to do something that requires that he learn a skill first, he will be motivated to apply himself. The students will be aware that they share in the responsibility for the school. They will be the central force in the school, and they will want to be with each other, hear each other, and will care about themselves and about each other. These are some of the characteristics that schools of the future may have. I hope we make the right choices today.

# Urban Integration: The Metropolitan Educational Park Concept

THOMAS F. PETTIGREW

Those who say educational desegregation is impossible and should be abandoned as a goal of American public schools are presently wrong but run the risk of becoming correct through a classic example of "the self-fulfilling prophecy." If we decide school desegregation in our cities cannot be achieved, we will surely act in such a manner as to make desegregation a most unlikely occurrence.

This paper explores one direction needed for desegregation of schools in our largest metropolitan areas. The metropolitan educational park offers an effective response to the chief structural supports of *de facto* school segregation; and it boasts many other appealing advantages. But it is no panacea. The park concept raises a number of difficulties which reveal clearly the need for careful planning of these enormously expensive centers.

Two proposals are advanced: the establishment of a Commission for Metropolitan Education; and the construction of a demographic simulation of the future dimensions of educational desegregation.

## I. The Problem

"This is our basic conclusion," states the National Advisory Commision on Civil Disorders flatly: "Our nation is moving toward two societies, one black, one white—separate and unequal."

Nothing about American public education refutes this stark conclusion. "Racial isolation in the schools," concludes the U.S. Commission on Civil Rights, "is intense whether the cities are large or small, whether they are located North or South."[1] Thus, in the fall of 1965, two-thirds of all Negro pupils in the first grade of public schools and one-half in the twelfth grade of public schools were enrolled in schools with 90 to 100 per cent Negro student bodies. Moreover, seven out of every eight Negro pupils in the first grade of public schools and two-thirds in the twelfth grade of public schools were enrolled in predominantly Negro schools.

Though different in magnitude, the regional discrepancies do not change the picture significantly—while 97 per cent of Negro first graders in the public schools of the urban South attended in 1965 predominantly Negro schools, the figure for the urban North was 72 per cent. White children are even more segregated. In the fall of 1965, 80 per cent of white public school children in both the first and twelfth grades were located in 90 to 100 per cent white schools.[2]

Moreover, the separation is increasing. In Cincinnati, for example, seven out of every ten Negro elementary children in 1950 attended predominantly Negro schools, but by 1965 nine out of ten did so. And while Negro elementary enrollment had doubled over these fifteen years, the number in predominantly Negro schools had tripled.[3] This pattern of growing separation is typical of American central cities, the very cities where Negro Americans are concentrated in greatest numbers.

There are at least four major causes for this growing pattern of de facto school segregation: (1) trends in racial demography; (2) the anti-metropolitan nature of school district organization; (3) the effects of private schools; and (4) intentional segregation similar to the older problem of de jure segregation.

The first two of these factors become apparent as soon as we compare public school organization and current racial demographic trends. There are approximately 27,000 school districts in the United States, with almost all of the recent consolidation of districts limited to the rural areas. Thus, there are over 75 school districts in the Boston metropolitan area and 96 in the Detroit metropolitan area.[4] There is pitifully little cooperation between central city and suburban school systems; and there are vast fiscal and social disparities between districts—especially central city and suburban. Add to this the fact that over 80 per cent of all Negro Americans who live in metropolitan areas reside in central cities, while over half of all white Americans who live in metropolitan areas reside in suburbs, and the racial separation by district becomes intense. Racial housing trends are not encouraging and offer no hope for relief of educational separation in the next generation.[5] Consequently, America would face an enormous problem of *de facto* school segregation even if there were no patterns of intradistrict separation by race.

But, of course, the nation also faces the task of overcoming sharp racial segregation within school districts. For example, 90 per cent or more of the central city enrollment of Negro elementary school children are found in 90 to 100 per cent Negro schools in: Richmond, Va., Atlanta, Little Rock, Memphis, Gary, Omaha, Washington, D.C., Tulsa, Oklahoma City, Baltimore, and Chicago. In cities with large Roman Catholic populations this intra-district segregation is unwittingly increased by the absorption of many white children into the parochial system. Since only about 6 per cent of Negro Americans are Roman Catholics,[6] a large Church school system necessarily limits the available pool of school-age white children for a central city public school system. In St. Louis and Boston, about two of every five white children go to private schools; and in Philadelphia, roughly three out of every five white children go to private schools.

In addition, the Hickses and Wallaces in American political life make the problem of intra-district segregation worse by openly advocating separation, careful misplacement and zone-drawing of new facilities, and steadfast refusal to take those measures which would at least begin to ease the problem. The Civil Rights Commission provides in its report two pointed examples from Chicago and Cincinnati of *de facto* segregation by design.[7] And bad-faith school resistance to racial change is, of course, blatantly demonstrated in much of the rural South—where almost one-fifth of all Negro Americans still reside.

But the public resistance of anti-Negro political figures gains the headlines, while the more important structural barriers (demographic trends, anti-metropolitan school district organization, and private school effects) are often the critical factors.

## II. How Can We Desegregate Schools?

Can we really desegregate our public schools? Is it possible to achieve effective racially and socio-culturally balanced student bodies? Are there any "ultimate solutions" for our big-city school systems? Is not integregation really a nice but impossible notion? What about Washington, D.C., Harlem, South Side Chicago?

Initially, we must make a clear distinction between *small-ghetto and big-ghetto situations*, for what is possible and useful in the former may well be counter-productive in the latter. The small-ghetto situation generally involves a city with less than a seventh or so of its public school population Negro. Its high schools and often even its junior high schools are naturally desegregated, and with good faith it can correct its elementary school segregation *within* its borders. There are many such communities throughout the United States, and together they account for a surprisingly large minority of Negro children. They should not be confused with the Washingtons and Harlems, as such apostles of segregationist doom as Joseph Alsop are given to do.

The elementary schools in these small-ghetto cities can usually be desgregated with a plan custom-styled to the system utilizing a unique combination of the following within-district methods: (1) the district-wide redrawing of school lines to maximize racial balance (positive gerrymandering); (2) the pairing of predominantly white and Negro schools along the borders of the Negro ghetto (the Princeton plan); and (3) a priority for and careful placement of new and typically larger schools outside of the ghetto (the rebuilding plan). If there is a need to desegregate at the junior or senior high levels, two other devices are often sufficient: (4) the alteration of "feeder" arrangements from elementary grades to junior highs and from junior highs to senior highs in order to maximize racial balance (the balanced feeder plan); and (5) the conversion of more schools into district-wide specialized institutions (the specialized school plan). Controversy is typically minimal because the small-ghetto situation can usually be accommodated without widespread subsidized transportation of students (bussing).

The real problems of implementation occur for the big-ghetto situation. The small-ghetto devices are generally mere band-aid remedies for the city system with a substantial and growing percentage of Negro students. Thus, pairing schools along the ghetto's borders would have to be repeated every few years as the ghetto expanded. Or a new school built outside of the ghetto last year may only result in a nearly all-Negro school within the ghetto next year. Even in Boston, with only 26 per cent non-whites in its public school system, a sophisticated redistricting plan for elementary schools would have only minor effects. In a computer-assisted system analysis, the ultimate limit of re-districting was tested with the rules that children in grades one through three would not be assigned more than a half mile from their homes and children in grades four through six not more than three-quarters of a mile. Yet the proportion of Boston's non-white elementary students attending predominantly non-white schools would only be reduced from 78 per cent to 66 per cent and for non-white junior high students, from 65 per cent to 50 per cent.[8] Clearly, for Boston—not to mention the really enormous ghetto cities of New York, Philadelphia, Washington, Chicago, and Los Angeles—more sweeping measures are required.

If the criteria for these sweeping measures are specified, the form and direction of future efforts begin to take shape. And these criteria were suggested earlier in the discussion of the causes of *de facto* school segregation. In planning for big-ghetto desegregation, larger educational complexes drawing from wide attendance areas will be essential. These attendance areas will generally have to include both central city and suburban territory in order to ensure the optimal stable racial mix. The sites for these facilities must not only be convenient to the mass transit network but must also be on racially "neutral turf." Such locations would avoid immediate public labeling of the school as "white" or "Negro."

Racial specifications are by no means the only criteria for future remedies. Public schools in our largest cities have lost their former preeminence as the innovative educational leaders. Berkeley, California, Newton and Brookline, Massachusetts, and a host of other smaller communities are now the pacesetters. Thus, the plans for the future should accent and facilitate innovation. Indeed, future public schools should possess facilities which could rarely be duplicated by expensive private schools if they are to compete effectively for the children of advantaged parents. Such arrangements, of course, will cost considerable money; thus, a final criterion must be significant Federal support of capital costs.

## III. The Metropolitan Educational Park

Several designs would meet these criteria; but we shall consider one design as illustrative. Ringing our major cities with educational parks, each of which serves both inner city and suburban students, offers one basic plan—*the metropolitan park plan*. Each park would be located on "neutral turf" in an inner-ring suburb or just inside the central city boundary;[9] and it would be so placed that the same spoke of the mass transit system could bring both outer-ring suburban children into the park and inner-city children out to it. The attendance area of each park would ideally cut out a metropolitan pie-slice containing a minimum of 12,000 to 15,000 public school students, with the thin end of the slice in the more densely populated central city and the thick end in the more sparsely populated suburbs.

But what incentive could generate the metropolitan cooperation necessary for such a plan? A number of systems have considered educational parks, but they usually find the capital costs prohibitive. Moreover, many systems are currently hard pressed for expansion funds—especially as referenda for school construction bonds continue to be defeated throughout the nation. Federal funding, then, on a massive scale will obviously be needed, though it must be dispersed in a far more careful and strategic manner than the everybody-gets-his-cut, "river and harbors bill" principle of the 1965 Elementary and Secondary Education Act. As long as alternate Federal funding for capital costs is available, many school systems—particularly those in bad faith—will not choose to join a metropolitan park plan. Therefore, future Federal construction grants must: (1) involve more than one urban district, and the consortium must always include the central city (note that any one park would not require the entire metropolitan area to join the proposal—though some co-ordination would be necessary, perhaps through review by each area's metropolitan planning commission); (2) require racial and social desegregation—and, hopefully, integration—in every school involved (metropolitan involvement makes this requirement feasible); and (3) exclude alternate routes for Federal building funds (though if the first two criteria are met, the proposal need not adopt the metropolitan park plan as the model).

A 15,000 student, forty to fifty million dollar park, 90 per cent of it paid by the Federal government, would be a powerful inducement. But is such Federal funding possible in the near future? The answer, as with many other domestic questions, rests with the final termination of the Viet Nam war. Once the conflict ends, economists will urge major domestic spending to take up the slack from the cutback in defense expenditures. Nothing like the Viet Nam war costs, of course, would become available for the domestic scene. Yet, at such a time, a two-billion-dollars-a-year school construction program—enough for building roughly forty parks annually—is not unlikely. Here lies both a great opportunity and an equally great danger. If the money is distributed in the easy fashion of the 1965 Education Act to individual school districts, the anti-metropolitan effects could be disastrous for both race relations and public education. Federal building money spent in such a manner would further insulate aloof suburbia and institutionalize *de facto* school segregation in the inner city for at least another half century. School construction money is likely to be made available by the Federal government after Viet Nam. The vital question is: What will be its form and effects?

The educational park idea is not a panacea; there can be elegantly effective and incredibly ineffective parks. Yet ample Federal funding combined with the nation's planning and architectural genius should be able to set a new standard and direction for public schools. This combination has successfully been applied to public facilities ranging from interstate highways to magnificent airports. Now the combination should be applied to the benefit of children.

From high-rise structures to multiple-unit campuses, educational parks themselves can be planned in a variety of ways. The most widely discussed design would involve a reasonably large tract of land (eighty to one hundred acres as a minimum) and no fewer than fourteen or fifteen schools serving grades from kindergarten through high school. One educator has visualized a campus design for 18,000 students consisting of two senior high, four junior high, and eight elementary schools.[10] If the park were to serve an especially densely populated section, it would be best if it did not include the entire grade spectrum so that it could still cover a reasonably expansive and heterogeneous attendance area. In general, however, an educational park resembles a public university. Both include a variety of educational programs for a large group of students of varying abilities. And like public universities in our major cities, some parks could consist of high-rise structures, and some could develop a more spacious campus atmosphere with numerous buildings. The metropolitan park, it is hoped, could usually follow the campus model, since sufficient space would generally be obtainable at suburban-ring locations.[11]

Apart from offering racial remedies, the metropolitan park concept has a number of distinct advantages. First, there are considerable savings that accrue from consolidation; centralized facilities, such as a single kitchen, need not be duplicated in each of the park's units. Savings on capital costs, too, would accrue from simultaneous building of many units at one location. These savings, however, do not necessarily mean that the total construction and operating costs would be less than those for the same student capacity spread out in traditional units. The advantage is that for essentially the same cost metropolitan parks could boast significantly better facilities than traditional schools. Consequently, each child would be receiving far more per educational dollar in the metropolitan park.

The improved centralized facilities of the park should maximize innovations and individualized instruction. It is difficult to institute new approaches to learning in old settings. A prime finding of social change research is that new norms are easier to introduce in new institutions. The metropolitan park offers a fresh and exciting setting that should encourage new educational techniques and attract the more innovative members of the teaching profession. In addition, the park presents a rare design opportunity for building innovation into the physical and social structures of the schools. This, of course, includes the latest equipment for aiding the teacher and the student. Centralization enhances this process, for example, by providing efficient concentration of all electronic information storage, retrieval, and console facilities. Yet such centralization of equipment should not be viewed as leading inevitably to a wide assortment of frightening Orwellian devices cluttering the school. Poor planning could lead to this result, but the accent should be on individualized instruction as the unifying and positive theme—a theme far more possible in the park design than in the present model of scattered "little red schoolhouses."

Many innovations made possible by the metropolitan park extend beyond the equipment realm. For instance, the teaching profession today suffers from being one of the most undifferentiated by rank of all professions, a characteristic which discourages a lifelong orientation to the field. While the medical profession has a graded rank order of roles from intern and resident to chief of a service, teachers must either enter administration and become principals or shift to more prestigious schools in order to move up the ladder. By concentrating a large number of teachers in a relatively small area, far more role differentiation becomes possible. Thus, a teacher might progress from an apprentice in a team-teaching situation, to a master teacher in a team, to a supervisor of master teachers, etc. Faculty concentration also allows more intensive, across-school in-service training and the formation of departments across schools with rankings within departments as in universities (e.g., a junior high history department consisting of all history teachers in the four or five junior highs on the campus).

Consider, too, the innovative possibilities for guidance counselors. One of the central role conflicts within this profession has pitted psychological therapy against academic and occupational counseling, treatment against advice and direction. The park presents an opportunity to alleviate this split role by differentiating it. Academic and occupational direction could continue to be the focus of guidance counselors working within the schools themselves; while therapy for disturbed youngsters could be centralized, together with an extensive health facility made possible by the larger scale. Indeed, public health facilities for children might well be attracted to the park and run in close collaboration with the schools.

Concentration of students also allows wider course offerings. Specialized classes, from playing the lute to seventeenth-century English literature, become economically possible when the students electing them are gathered from units throughout the park. Moreover, concentration makes possible some remarkable facilities that can be shared by all of the park's units—e.g., an Olympic-sized swimming pool, extensive auditorium and theatrical equipment, etc. These special facilities could far surpass what is now available in all but the most affluent districts, become a source of student and community pride, and provide a competitive status advantage over private schools. They also would be used efficiently, rather than the minimal use expensive facilities receive in single-site schools.

The metropolitan park offers unusual opportunities for an effective liaison with a local university or college. Nova, the extensive educational park near Fort Lauderdale, Florida, even plans to include college and graduate work right on its campus. But direct contiguity is not necessary to develop a mutually beneficial coordination.

Recall that an important cause of public school segregation in many central cities is the enrollment of large percentages of white children in parochial schools. This fact suggests closer co-operation between public and parochial schools, and the metro-politan educational park could facilitate such cooperation under optimal conditions. Most parochial systems are currently in seri-ous financial condition and tapping into the park's superior facil-ities should prove attractive. Roman Catholic educators point out that those items that cost the most—the physical science labora-tories, gymnasium, and stadium—tend to be least related to the "moral training" that they believe to be the distinctive feature of their schools. Scattered site schools, public and parochial, make "shared time" and other cooperative arrangements awkward at best. And when parochial students come to take their public school class as a group, such segregation often reaps its usual harvest of intergroup tension and hostility.

A recent idea from Vermont introduces a more promising pos-sibility. At the time of planning a large educational park, Roman Catholic educators are provided the opportunity of buying an adjoining plot of land and constructing a new facility of their own. As long as the land price is consistent with its true value, no constitutional infringements appear to be involved. The new parochial facility need only concentrate on housing courses di-rectly needed for "moral training." Parochial pupils would be free as individuals, not as separated groups, to cross the park's grass, not urban streets, and attend physical education, science, and other public school courses when they fit their particular sched-ules. The Vermont plan offers construction and operating savings to hard-pressed parochial systems; and it offers a greater race and class student balance to hard-pressed public systems.[12]

Cost efficiency, educational innovations, more individualized instruction, wider course offerings, special facilities, and coordi-nation with universities and parochial schools—all of these ad-vantages of the well-designed metropolitan park are features that parents, white and Negro, would welcome in the schools of tomorrow. This is politically critical, for desegregation efforts of the past have seldom come as intrinsic parts of a larger package promising an across-the-board improvement in education for *all* children.

## IV. Objections to the Park

In addition to the natural resistance to change, four major objections have been raised to the park concept: (1) excessive capital costs; (2) the phasing-out of existing schools; (3) the problem of impersonalization in the large complexes; and (4) the loss of neighborhood interest and involvement in the school. Each is a serious objection and deserves comment.

The park *is* expensive, and major Federal funding is necessary. Furthermore, mistakes in design and location could be disastrous. A park is an enormous commitment of resources, and, if poorly conceived, it could stand for years as a major mistake in planning. This is precisely what would happen if parks were operated totally within central city systems, for demographic projections prove the folly of building parks for a single central city system as a desegregation device.[13] It is for this reason that the parks of the future must be *metropolitan* in character.

Present schools were expensive, too, and raise the problem of phasing out existing facilities. For many urban districts this is not a problem; they already have over-utilized schools with double shifts and rising enrollments or old schools long past their usefulness. But some urban districts have many new schools and would be hesitant to join a park consortium. The program, however, is a long-term one. It is hoped that by the early 1970's most of the nation's leading metropolitan areas would boast one or more parks; these in turn could serve as models for completing the park rings in the decade. Moreover, elementary and secondary student enrollments will rise rapidly: from 48.4 million in 1964 to a projected 54.9 million in 1974 and 66 million in the fateful year of 1984.[14] Metropolitan parks, then, could be phased in as older facilities are phased out and enrollments swiftly rise.

Such a process would be ideal nationally, but there will be special problems in localities with "planned *de facto* school segregation." These are cities, such as Chicago, which in recent years have purposely built new schools in the heart of their Negro ghettos in order to maximize racial separation. If racial progress is to be made in these cities, recent structures will have to be converted to new uses—perhaps, to much-needed community centers.

The third objection to parks centers upon the impersonalization of organizational bigness—"the Kafka problem." Indeed, much of the park's description—15,000 students, a staff approaching 1,000, the latest electronic equipment—has a frightening Kafka ring; and one can easily imagine how an ill-designed park could justify these fears. But such a prospect is not inherent in the park plan; nor is bigness a park problem alone, for many of today's huge urban high schools accommodate many thousands of students in a single unit and arouse the same uneasiness. In fact, imaginatively designed parks could act to counter the urban trend toward ever-larger public school units. *Smaller* schools at each level can be economically built as units within the park; and careful planning can afford a reasonable degree of privacy for each unit while still providing access to the shared facilities of the park.

Some critics are particularly concerned about the park's loss of neighborhood interest and involvement. The criticism assumes that most urban public schools today are neighborhood-based, and that they generate considerable neighborhood involvement. Serious doubts can be raised about both assumptions: we may well be worrying about the loss of something already lost. In any event, there is no evidence to indicate that only a neighborhood-based school can generate parental concern, or that a metropolitan park could not duplicate this feat, or that there is a close and negative association between the size of the attendance area and involvement.

The criticism does raise an important planning issue: How can the park be initiated and planned to heighten parental and community interest? Certainly, the special facilities, the university-liaison, and cooperation with parochial schools could help generate community pride and interest. So could smaller schools and a park school board of parents with wide authority short of taxing power. Furthermore, widespread use of the park for adult education, community affairs, etc., would also contribute to public involvement; indeed, the special facilities of the park lend themselves to such adult use more readily than the typical school today.

Finally, one might ask how such a metropolitan educational park plan fits with other such widely discussed possibilities as "decentralization" and "community schools." First, it should be noted that decentralization and community control are typically advanced either apart from integration considerations or as outright alternatives to integration. "The Bundy Report" for New York City, for instance, could well lead to racially homogeneous districts that would institutionalize racial segregation for generations to come. Yet there is an obvious need in such large and unwieldy systems as New York and Chicago to decentralize authority, as well as a general need to increase parental and community involvement in public education.

Similar to compensatory education, however, these possibilities acquire force and meaning when they *accompany* the drive for integration rather than substitute for it. Thus, effective decentralization need not take the form of isolated social class or racial islands, but should assume the metropolitan pie-slice shapes described earlier as ideal attendance areas for educational parks. New York City's schools *could* be organized along the lines suggested by "The Bundy Report" in such a way as to help rather than hinder integration.[15]

In summary, then, those who say there is nothing we can do about the educational segregation of our major cities are fortunately wrong. This is not to say that desegregation progress will be easy, or even that we will do what is necessary to achieve such progress. But it is to say that it potentially *can* be done for a significant number of urban Americans, white and Negro.


## V. Two Proposals

Among the proposals which flow from this discussion are an ambitious effort to establish a Commission for Metropolitan Education and a more modest attempt to construct a demographic simulation of the future of educational desegregation. Each of these proposals deserves discussion.

## A. A COMMISSION FOR METROPOLITAN EDUCATION

Either established by a single large foundation or a consortium of foundations interested in education, an action-oriented Commission for Metropolitan Education is imperative to set the model for Federal efforts in education after the Viet Nam war. If it were adequately budgeted and staffed, this Commission could pursue a range of significant thrusts markedly different from such ill-fated and unfortunate private programs as the Ford Foundation's Great Cities compensatory education endeavor or its present "community control" program in three New York City schools.

First, and most important, the Commission could experiment in the making of strategic grants to metropolitan consortia for a variety of cross-district cooperative schemes. Remarkably little cooperation exists today between districts within metropolitan areas, even in such obvious areas of mutual benefit as common procurement of supplies. The "Great High School" plans of Pittsburgh, for instance, have been drawn up with virtually no communication with surrounding suburban districts. Not even the richest nation on earth in peacetime can expect to fund adequately over 25,000 separate school districts that largely compete against each other.

Multi-district grants should make quality education for *all* of a metropolitan area's children its primary goal, keeping a careful check that this includes expanding opportunities for racial and class integration. At the present this focus would mean, among other possibilities, support for the spread of Boston's METCO and Hartford's Project Concern to other metropolitan areas. Though transporting relatively small numbers of Negro children to empty seats in suburban schools offers no long-term solution in itself, it represents the beginnings of metropolitan cooperation, helps to mobilize metropolitan thinking and political pressures, and, as in Massachusetts, may lead to planning for state-operated demonstration schools in urban areas.

As indicated throughout this paper, public-parochial school coordination should be a focus of the Commission. Especially in such cities as Philadelphia and St. Louis, where large proportions of the school-aged white children attend church-schools, the Commission could encourage new and more meaningful methods of joint operation. High in priority among these methods would be those involving physical proximity of public and private facilities and individual, rather than group, participation of parochial students in public programs.

A Commission for Metropolitan Education would have many points of entry and leverage. One is provided for by the new Model Cities program. Though Congress stripped the program of metropolitan and desegregation *requirements*, it nevertheless presents *opportunities* to lay the groundwork for these goals. Relatively small but carefully designed grants to critical local agencies working with Model Cities planning in particular cities could exploit this possibility. In this regard, the metropolitan planning councils that exist in most urban areas make promising starting points.

Another point of entry and leverage is the university. Urban study programs at Chicago, Columbia, Harvard, and other universities in major centers have already received significant foundation funding and provide bases for both research and direct involvement of higher education. The Commission could ensure that metropolitan educational concerns not be left out of the work and action of these urban programs; this means at the minimum that the schools of education at these institutions be directly linked organizationally to, and be given responsibility for drawing up, operational proposals for local metropolitan coordination.

Still another point of entry is through the architectural, design, and planning professions. Large educational complexes, whether in the park form described here or not, are definitely in the future. They could be enormous monuments to poor planning; or they could introduce an entirely new and upgraded level of facility for public education. So critical, then, is the effective use of America's best architectural and planning genius, the Commission might well assign a high priority to this area. Special grants to innovative members of these professions for work with educators in creating a range of skillful designs to meet varied situations and specifications could prepare the ground for effective utilization of the Federal school construction funds of the post-Viet Nam future.

Plans, no matter how imaginative, are never as convincing as the concrete example. This suggests that the Commission should invest in the development of at least one well-conceived metropolitan educational complex. There is actually no metropolitan complex in existence today meeting the criteria discussed in this paper, so that any such model development would undoubtedly receive considerable attention. To increase its impact, the complex should be located in an area where racial and class issues exist in a not too atypical form. Thus, Washington, D.C. and New York City on one end and Salt Lake City and Spokane on the other would not be ideal hosts for this model venture. More typical would be, say, Providence, where interest in the idea has already developed throughout the metropolitan area, state educational officials are favorable, and the Negro population percentage is similar to that of all but the heaviest centers of concentration.

Finally, the Commission might well consider establishing a land bank of ideal metropolitan sites for future educational complexes. Such an effort could consist of interest-free loans to school district consortia to purchase strategic sites for building metropolitan complexes in the future. Ask urban superintendents with long-range views about such sites, and they will immediately provide you with one or more ideal locations which could be purchased if only the capital funds were available. Ask urban planners about such sites, and they are likely to tell you that such locations are in short supply and rapidly disappearing—especially in the older Eastern cities. These opinions suggest that a land bank of even modest proportions might prove of critical significance.

## B. A DEMOGRAPHIC SIMULATION OF THE FUTURE DIMENSIONS OF EDUCATIONAL DESEGREGATION

Much of today's debate over the public education of Negro American children resembles the proverbial blind men describing the elephant. Each commentator generalizes broadly from his own limited slice of the problem. Yet the critical context for any intelligent approach to the issue is basically demographic. Integration ideologists make it sound as if total school desegregation could be accomplished next fall if it were not for such resisters as Wallace and Hicks. Most observers of the urban scene can eye the growing densities of Negro population in central cities and cast aside such contentions as naïve. But the same observers are susceptible to an equally naïve reading of racial demography that characterizes virtually all educational integration efforts as futile.

Earlier it was noted that Negro Americans are represented in the nation's metropolitan areas in a similar proportion to that of white Americans—about two of every three. And it was noted that Washington, D.C. and Harlem are *not* typical of Negro communities throughout urban America. In addition to these oversights, the apostles of demographic doom must also: (1) assume that Negro ghettos will not extend into suburbs (as Pittsburgh's eastern ghetto already has and Chicago's western ghetto is about to); (2) project that the single-site model of so-called "neighborhood" schools will dominate future school plans despite its increasingly uneconomic future; (3) contend that the overwhelmingly white parochial systems in key central cities will not cooperate more and more with public systems; (4) hold that virtually all school district and municipal boundaries will remain as they are; and (5) maintain that metropolitan cooperation in public education will not grow despite its economic attractions and the possibility of future Federal incentives. None of these sweeping assumptions appears fully justified.

As usual, the truth seems to lie somewhere in between the two extreme interpretations. On the one hand, with all the good faith, metropolitan cooperation, and Federal construction funds imaginable, school integration as a realistic alternative for virtually all urban Negroes is a long-term goal. On the other hand, vastly expanded integrated education in metropolitan America is not only possible but could be achieved by means of devices known now. Yet these two statements do not delimit the problem sufficiently. How many urban Negroes and whites could be integrated with various alternations in present school organization? What would be the Negro demand for such integration? What would be the Negro demand for separate schools? And what is the range of possible answers to these queries for 1980, 1990, or 2000? While no precise estimates are possible, current thinking is now unaided by even the order of magnitude and range of possibilities. With the growing technology of computer-assisted simulation of social processes, however, work on these issues would be valuable for planning not just in education but in all realms of American race relations.

We know enough now to realize that the resulting models would be complex. For example, Negro demand for integration is not just a simple function of central city concentration but is highly dependent upon the realistic opportunities available for integration. Not unlike the increase in total automobile travel attracted by new turnpikes, any model would have to contain feedback components of ever-increasing integrationist demand with expanding actual integration. Likewise, it would be necessary to have estimates of rising demand for racial separatism with increased segregation. Recall the Civil Rights Commission data on Negro and white adults which strongly suggest that adult interracial behavior, as well as interracial attitudes, are importantly a function of integrated or segregated school experience. Recall, too, the surprisingly favorable response of lower-status Negro parents to having their children participate in Hartford's Project Concern and integrated schools once it became a viable possibility. But these data are rare. Hence, such a full-scale simulation project would not only provide a valuable context for political decision but would also lead to significant research aimed at providing the model with values for its vital parameters.

REFERENCES

1. This section constitutes in large part a terse restatement of Chapters 1 and 2 of: U.S. Commission on Civil Rights, *Racial Isolation in the Public Schools*, Vols. I and II, Washington, D.C.: U.S. Government Printing Office, 1967. The quote is taken from Volume I, page 7.
2. J. S. Coleman *et al.*, *Equality of Educational Opportunity*, Washington, D.C.: U.S. Government Printing Office, 1966, pp. 3-7.
3. U.S. Commission on Civil Rights, op. cit. Vol. I, page 8.
4. Ibid. p. 17.
5. K. E. Taeuber and Alma F. Taeuber, *Negroes in Cities*, Chicago: Aldine, 1965.
6. N. Glenn, "Negro Religion and Negro Status in the United States," in L. Schneider, ed., *Religion, Culture and Society*, New York: Wiley, 1964, pp. 623-639.
7. U.S. Commission on Civil Rights, op. cit. Vol. I, pp. 48-49.
8. Joint Center for Urban Studies of M.I.T. and Harvard, "Changes in School Attendance Districts as a Means of Alleviating Racial Imbalance in the Boston Public Schools," Unpublished report, August 1966.
9. Other convenient and racially-neutral sites would be appropriate to specialized metropolitan educational parks. Rather than near the central city and suburban boundary, sites near the art museum, the science center, the music center, and colleges and universities could possess enough appeal and status to attract suburban children into the central city despite the longer commuting.
10. G. Brain, "The Educational Park: Some Advantages and Disadvantages," in N. Jacobson, ed., *An Exploration of the Educational Park Concept*, New York: New York Board of Education, 1964, p. 16.
11. In some of the thickly populated metropolitan areas, especially the older cities of the East, ideal sites are already scarce and rapidly disappearing. Hence, the recommendation below for parksite land banks.
12. The old stereotype of parochial school students as children of working-class immigrants is just that—an outdated stereotype. Roman Catholic children who comprise the students for the Church-

operated educational systems tend as a group to be distinctly
higher in socio-economic background than Roman Catholic children who attend the public systems. Thus, inclusion of parochial
pupils in public school courses and programs is likely to facilitate
social class as well as racial balance.

13. The Philadelphia Urban League, in proposing non-metropolitan
    parks for a central city system the majority of whose student body
    is already non-white, has advanced just such a plan.

14. F. Keppel, *The Necessary Revolution in American Education*,
    New York: Harper and Row, 1966, p. 19.

15. Private communication from Professor Dan Dobson of New York
    University. Of course, *no* decentralization and redistricting plan
    in New York City can solve the problem of desegregation alone.
    The point is only that it can be made to seal in racial and class
    segregation or to improve slightly the situation depending on how
    it is accomplished.

# The Changing Nature of Vocational Guidance

DONALD E. SUPER

Change which would once have taken place over a span of three or four generations now takes place in less than one lifetime.

Looking ahead, more than half of our students are to have discontinuous careers. They will occupy, during the course of their working lives, a series of unrelated and often depersonalized positions, and the continuity in their careers is not that of a field of work; it is that of a person working. Those who pursue discontinuous careers will need to know when to change and will need the skills and understanding which make possible quick training for, or adaptation to, a new type of work.

What, then, becomes of career guidance which must recognize the continuity of the individual and seek to help him find this continuity even in the midst of change? No one as yet has all of the answers to this question. Too few have even asked it.

## I. Change

More than two hundred years ago, with the Enlightenment, Man began effectively to proclaim the dignity of Man, and the last hundred years have seen the increasingly rapid disappearance of personal service occupations or their transformation into the depersonalized large-scale service which now characterizes the work of the laundryman, the barber, and the cleaning woman. About one hundred years ago Man began inventing agricultural machinery, and the past fifty years have seen a steady decline in the numerical importance of agricultural workers. Nearly fifty years ago Man created the assembly line, and the resulting substitution of obsolescence and junking for maintenance and repair began to put the craftsman out of business both as producer and as repairman. Much less than twenty-five years ago the electronic computer was developed, and today we are witnessing the disappearance of the semiskilled worker, whether machine tender or record keeper, as automation does his work more rapidly and more accurately.

As time passes, the rate of change increases, each change contributing to the speeding up of the next change. Change which would once have taken place over a span of three or four generations now takes place in less than one lifetime: the grandchildren of people who first saw the *Clermont* steam up the Hudson River, sailed round the Horn in Yankee clippers; but some of us, who still remember when electricity began to displace gas as a source of light, now help carry out the electronic revolution of which automation is but the most dramatic and most drastic element.

With automation we now have much better means for studying manpower needs and for forecasting employment trends. But because of automation we have less adequate data to put into our computers. The abolition of ancient and honorable, if not so honorific, types of work in factories and in offices and the creation of a limited number of new and demanding occupations leave us uncertain as to the future which awaits the large majority of persons who, in the past, have filled the routine and semi-routine positions which employed the bulk of our manpower.

It is easy to predict, as automated equipment takes over the control of both the processes of manufacturing and the keeping of the records of production and distribution, that production and clerical jobs will decrease rapidly and dramatically. It is easy to foresee that, in the same way, many routine distributive occupations will disappear as automated stock control and sales equipment move consumer products and handle sales.

But it is not so easy to predict what the factory operatives, office workers, and store clerks who are displaced by automation, or the young people who might, a decade earlier, have entered these fields of employment, will do to earn a living. The common prediction, we have all heard, is that service occupations will expand and develop, that new jobs will open up in fields such as recreation, health, and perhaps even maintenance, repair, and some of the luxury crafts which society will again see fit to support even while providing a high standard of mass-produced living for all. It would be gratifying to be able to obtain the services of a real gardener to take care of a lawn and flower beds. It would be good to have one's old hi-fi set repaired and revamped (because one happens to like it), rather than junked because of the unavailability or high cost of competent service men and the relative ease of producing new models. It would be good to be able to buy, for a new house, a colonial mantelpiece which is not exactly like seven out of ten other colonial mantelpieces in other new houses.

But how am I, how are you, who are among the fortunate who are not so likely to be displaced by automation, going to support the additional recreation staff, the expanded health services, the gardener, the electronics repairman, and the woodcarver or millwork man? How can you and I, in good conscience, encourage boys and girls to think in terms of such jobs before our affluent society devises ways of using its great productive capacity to support them? Will those of us who still render services which are deemed essential in our present economy be paid so well, thanks to the productivity of automated agriculture and manufacturing, thanks to the efficiency of automated distribution and record keeping, that we will be able to employ, either on our own payrolls or in the tax-supported public service, the hundreds of thousands of displaced semiskilled and unskilled workers? Will the productive and distributive systems themselves be used directly to support these expanded service fields? No one can pretend to know, at present.

The prediction that the service occupations will provide the new opportunities of the future is therefore not a prediction, in the strict sense of the word, but a hope. In counseling concerning vocational choice and in providing training opportunities in the service fields, then, we must recognize that we are playing, not with probabilities, but with hopes. In underlining this fact I do not mean to denigrate hope; I merely consider it important to recognize clearly with what it is that we are dealing.

## II. Uncertainty

It is with *uncertainty* that the counselor deals, uncertainty in the occupational structure and uncertainty in the careers of individuals. There is a certain amount of irony in the fact that *I* am stressing this, for one of the principal findings of the longitudinal study of vocational development in which I have been engaged for a dozen years is that the essence of vocational maturity is *planfulness.* The result is that I find myself defining the task of the counselor as two seemingly incompatible activities: the development of planfulness and planning in students, and the recognition of the fact that, for most students, planning is becoming increasingly difficult and perhaps impossible. Let us focus first on the uncertainties of the occupational structure and then deal with those of the individual's career.

### OCCUPATIONAL UNCERTAINTIES

One of the baffling problems which counselors face in dealing with occupational information is the uncertainty of society as to how much economic planning should be done, with a resulting vacillation and mixing of economic policies. Our society prides itself on its free-enterprise system, while restraining the successful entrepreneur from crowning his success by the creation of a monopoly; we permit our privately owned rail transport system to deteriorate in its own not-so-sweet way, while helping motor transport by building highways and air transport through a variety of subsidies; we balk at government ownership of the means of production and distribution, but we prime the economic pump by reducing taxes. Perhaps this combination of public control or planning and of lack of control or clear plans is best. As I am not an economist, I can hardly pretend to say, although one could quote economists in support of a variety of positions. Planning in the economic realm, and specifically occupational forecasting, is difficult even for specialists, as the manpower situation in the mid-1960's in Soviet Russia showed. The data made available to counselors and students are therefore incomplete, unclear, and often irrelevant.

Let us take, for example, the prediction that young people who will, patently, *not* be absorbed by factory or clerical occupations, will find new opportunities in recreation, in health, and in service occupations. Does this mean that Jane Smith, high school senior who graduated in June, hoping to get a job as a file clerk, will not get such a job, but will be able to get one in recreation? Or does it apply only to next year's or the next decade's seniors? Does it mean that John Jones, who aims to study to be an office machine repairman after graduation should, instead, look for a school in which he can study computer installation and maintenance? No one knows, although we can with some certainty say that it may mean these things for a few people this year and for increasing numbers in future years. We are still left, however, with the unanswerable question of just how many and who are the few.

CAREER UNCERTAINTIES

But let us focus on the more psychological issue, the question of the uncertainties in the career of the individual.

The term "career" is much misused in vocational guidance, and its misuse reflects a serious bias in counselors. The bias in question is one of which we have heard much in recent years, but the nature of which is still often misunderstood. I refer to the middle-class bias.

Consider these words for a moment. "Bias," the evil that made possible anti-Semitism and the Nazi excesses, the evil that underlies discrimination as we know it in America, is a bad word in today's vocabulary. By a curious process of association, however, good words juxtaposed with bad words themselves acquire an evil connotation, even though there may be nothing evil about what they denote. The words "middle class" have, by association, now acquired a bad connotation. But there is nothing wrong with being middle class—nothing, that is, that is any more wrong than there is with being upper or lower class. In fact, there is a good deal of evidence which shows that there is more that is right with being middle class than with being anything else. The middle class, with all its very real defects, *has* been demonstrated to do better in child rearing than either the upper or the lower classes, to supply a larger proportion of entrants into socially significant occupations than do other classes, and in other ways to provide more generally desirable citizens.

We live in a predominantly middle-class society, which means that the process of socialization in the home and in the school is one which might, if you will pardon the play on words, be called middle-classification. It is the process of equipping children and adolescents to live in a middle-class society, according to middle-class values. Again, there is nothing wrong in being middle class, and there is much that is right in middle-class values. The fact that we suffer from a middle-class orientation is to be deplored, not just because of certain real defects of middle classishness, but particularly because of the bad effects of failing, as a result of this orientation, to recognize some important facts and to take them into account. The orientation has resulted in a bias. If, as many cultural anthropologists would agree, a major objective of education in our society is to induct people into the great middle class, we would do a better job of it if we were free of the bias while keeping our orientation, if we were equipped with a clear understanding of people who are not middle class and of ways of life which differ from those of the middle class.

This middle-class bias, to come back to my theme, has typically led educators in general and counselors in particular to give one of the two acceptable vocational definitions to the word "career" and to forget the other equally acceptable definition. Webster defines a career as *first,* a course of continued progress in the life of a person, a nation, or other entity, and *second,* as a field for the pursuit of consecutive progressive achievement. It is this latter sense which has been widely adopted by counselors and personnel men, as when we refer to career fields in the armed forces or to making a career in business; in this sense, career has come to be almost a synonym for occupation, and

the connotation is one of a person entering an occupation, finding in it a major means of self-actualization, and staying in it for
the balance of his working life. This is a concept which has valid-
ity for a number of people, including physicians who typically
remain in medicine from medical school until retirement and
businessmen who climb from the position of junior executive
toward, if not to, that of president of the corporation. But these
careers with continuity and self-fulfillment possibilities, these
*stable* and *conventional careers*, as they have come to be called
in occupational sociology, characterize only about half of our
working population. The other half (and hence the emphasis in
my talk) have *unstable* or *multiple-trial* careers. That is, they
occupy, during the course of their working lives, a series of unrelated and often depersonalized positions, and the continuity in
their careers is not that of field work, it is that of a person working. Another way of putting it is to say that whereas about half
of our labor force has what might be called a *life work*, the
other half has a *life of work*.

And why is giving the word "career" the occupational, rather
than the personal, meaning illustrative of a middle-class bias?
Because it is the middle class who tend to have stable and conventional careers (about 60 percent of our population in the
past, actually, although some authorities say it will soon be only
30 percent) and the lower classes who tend to have unstable and
multiple-trial careers (about 40 percent of the labor force in the
past and some 70 percent in the future). It is in the professions,
the executive, the skilled, and the clerical fields, that the continuity has typically been found. It is in the semiskilled and
unskilled employment that is entered by the majority of persons
from lower socio-economic levels that discontinuity is typical. In
thinking of careers as involving continuity and self-concept implementation in an occupational field, counselors reflect an
awareness of middle-class career patterns and a lack of awareness of lower-class career patterns; they reflect, that is, a middle-
class bias.

It is important, here, to make a distinction between the blind
assumption of the appropriateness of the middle-class career pat-

tern for all persons, and the thoughtful conclusion that a middle-
class career pattern is an objective which might best be sought
by all. Perhaps stable and conventional careers *are* the most desirable, in view of the fact that they provide greater continuity,
make possible more detailed and more effective planning, provide a sounder basis for family financing, and tend to permit
self-fulfillment. They may, therefore, be desirable goals for all,
just as the taking on and achievement of middle-class values
seems, despite their defects, a legitimate goal of education in a
society such as ours. But the fact of desirability for all does not
mean attainability for all, at least not so long as our economy is
based in part on a large number of jobs which can be filled by
semi-transient, easily replaced, anonymous workers.

Stabilized neither by their own investment in the acquisition
of a skill, nor by the challenge of their work, nor by the rewards
of their efforts, large numbers of the semiskilled and unskilled
move from job to job in search of better working conditions, of
work which provides more assurance of continuity, or better out-
lets for ability and interest. But workers who can be let go when
a job is finished or an order is filled, and who can easily be replaced when production is to be resumed, cannot have stable or
conventional careers unless the productive and distributive systems are organized to provide them continuity. For most unskilled and semiskilled workers, including office clerks, and for
increasing numbers of young people for whom automated business and industry have no place, a career with middle-class stability and continuity is a will-o'-the-wisp. The reality, for the 50
or 70 percent, is discontinuity, uncertainty, and change.


III. Guidance for Discontinuity

If more than half of our students are to have discontinuous careers, judging by past experience, and if the unpredictables of
automation mean that change and uncertainty are to characterize the lives of an even greater percentage, what then becomes
of career guidance? Do we declare that it is for the elite only,

and let placement in a job when available and needed take its place for the 50 percent, for the majority of the future? Or do we, recognizing the facts of career patterns, develop a type of career guidance and of vocational education which recognizes the continuity of the individual and seeks to help him find this continuity even in the midst of change?

To do the former, and guide only the elite, will hardly satisfy us in this day and age. The able and ambitious may, and do, need special kinds of information and experience, but not consideration to the exclusion of others. To guide the development of all students is the only acceptable policy, but it will not be easy, for we need a new philosophy of career guidance and of vocational education which not only is strange to most educators, but which is easily distorted into a repugnant snobbishness.

What will be the essential characteristics of this novel type of career guidance and of the new vocational education of which it will be a part? No one as yet has all of the answers to this question. Too few have even asked it, and those who have are more conscious of the gaps in our knowledge than of the content with which to fill them. But, since work we all must, today as well as tomorrow, with whatever knowledge and insight we now have, let us see what we can marshal in the way of a concept of guidance for discontinuous careers.

*First,* counselors and students, and the classroom teachers with whom they work, need an understanding of the types and characteristics of career patterns and life stages as described in Miller and Form's *Industrial Sociology*[1] and in my *Psychology of Careers,*[2] and particularly of the unstable and multiple-trial career patterns and the characteristics of people whose careers tend to fall into these two categories.

*Second,* they need an understanding of what discontinuity and change in a rapidly evolving economy means in the way of adaptability and retraining. The obsolescence of the methods of production and distribution, and even of the very scientific principles upon which some methods are based, calls for expanding the scope and duration of education on a scale such as has never until recently been dreamed of, for varieties of occupations such

as we have never seen, and for education continuing or resumed
at times and over a longer period of time than any but a few
scholarly professional men have ever experienced. Whereas even
today the label "retread" implies some inadequacy on the part
of the person needing to be retrained or brought up-to-date, before long it will be the person who believes he has not needed
retraining who will be suspect, on the grounds that either he or
his occupation has stood still to the point of fossilization. Sometimes the retraining will be refresher or remodeling training, because of advances in the substance or techniques of the occupation, and sometimes it will be training in a new field of work
because of the decline or disappearance of the old.

*Third,* we must rid ourselves of the idea that non-academic
students do not need academic subjects. Or perhaps it would be
better to say that we must recognize that the academic subjects
taught in high school are *not* academic, but basic. Please do not
mistake me, I am no Essentialist, no academic snob or cultural
ethnocentric who thinks that those who are not interested in
learning what he learned, in the way in which he learned it, are
unworthy of a teacher's attention. What I mean is that linguistic
and arithmetic skills, and scientific, economic, political, and social
understanding, are essential vocational skills for all students. This
is so even for those who will leave school before graduation
(whether in order to escape from school or in order to go to
work), *especially* for those who will drop out or who will not
continue beyond high school. For these are the students who,
pursuing discontinuous careers, will need to know when to
change and how to change, and who will need the skills and
understanding which make possible quick training for, or adaptation to, a new type of work. For those who need retraining for
a new type of work, languages, mathematics, and natural sciences
often prove to be basic vocational skills; for those who must
change type or location of work, economics (the economics of
occupations and of unemployment, a science of vocational economics which is still non-existent), and psychology and sociology
(the psychology and sociology of work, of organizations, of occupations, of careers, and of leisure) are essential subjects.

*Fourth,* counselors, curriculum makers, and teachers need to recognize the facts of geographic mobility. These are two-fold in nature: first, many people today move from one part of the country to another in search of employment or of a suitable way of life, as we see most dramatically in the cotton fields of Mississippi and in the industrial cities of the Middle West and West Coast; and secondly, most movement is, surprisingly, within a relatively small geographic area well represented by the county. For every cotton or mountain county which exports its economically unassimilable youth and adults, there is a Middletown like that of my current New York State study, in which two-thirds of the high school freshmen of 1951-1952 now, after finishing their military service and college study in various parts of the country, live within a two-hour drive of Middletown. This means that the occupational information which the counselor needs to use and to disseminate and the conditions for which the schools need to educate and train youth are both those of the home market and those of the export market. Some farmers' sons will continue to farm, while others will move to nearby towns, and still others will move to more remote cities; some daughters of factory workers will work in nearby factories, but others will work in downtown offices, and still others will demonstrate new cosmetic products or modern methods of baby care in distant centers. The geographic mobility and the economic changes of contemporary America mean that the educator in Cleveland or in Charleston must collect and use information concerning life and work not only in the Cuyahoga, the Ohio, and the Monongahela valleys, but also in the Appalachicola, the Columbia River, and the San Joaquin valleys.

Please note that I have said not only work, but life and work, for one fact which has become clear in work with people transplanted from the tobacco fields of North Carolina to the slums of Chicago is that many of them need education in the ways of city life, in such rudimentary matters as methods of getting from one part of the city to another (there is no Loop in Goldsboro) and of garbage disposal (trash accumulates faster and remains longer in a Chicago street than in a Carolina pine barren). This

kind of education in urban living is, in a very real sense, vocational education—for how is a man to get a city job unless he
knows how to travel in the city, and how is he to keep the city
job, if he cannot manage everyday living in the city? In the case
of foreign diplomats and overseas scholars and students we recognize these needs, organizing orientation courses in which both
husbands and wives learn about shopping twice or three times a
day in France, employing a domesticated brigand to patrol the
garden at night in Burma, or getting work done despite allowing
time for a siesta in Spain. But in the case of our potentially mo-
bile school boys and girls, many of whom make moves right here
on our continent which are just as dramatic as those just referred to, we leave such things to chance.

THE IRRELEVANCE OF HIGH SCHOOL FOR SOME

What I have been saying *seems* to contain, as we must recognize, a grave inherent contradiction. For I have been saying, on
the one hand, that our generally accepted ideas of education and
of vocational guidance are inappropriate for most of our students, and I have been affirming, on the other, the importance of
the traditional basic subjects which have generally been taught
for middle-class, college-bound students. Is the contradiction
real? If not, why not?

It has frequently been claimed, during the past two decades,
that much of what the high schools do is not meaningful to boys
and girls from the lower socio-economic levels. A. B. Hollingshead,[3] Allison Davis,[4] W. Lloyd Warner,[5] and others have docu-
mented and proclaimed the fact. Furthermore, they have pointed
out that much of what might be meaningful is denied meaning
by the middle-class attitudes and values of teachers and of the
socially and politically dominant pupils and their parents. At the
same time, technological change and occupational trends actually make the basic, therefore abstract, and consequently im-
portant-in-an-uncertain-future-rather-than-today subjects of the
high school essential for the boy and girl of lesser ability and
more humble status whose upbringing and capacities make it

more difficult for them to see the importance of that which is not immediately useful.

These boys and girls can, given appropriate experiences, see the importance of these subjects. In my longitudinal study of boys in Middletown, N.Y., nearly half of the boys who dropped out of high school had, by the time they were twenty-five years old, obtained a high school diploma either in course, or, more frequently, by examination; when reinterviewed at age twenty-five a number of dropouts discussed their discovery of the need for good grounding in communication and mathematical skills. Some described how they had gone about trying to make up for lost time in these areas, while others lamented the fact that, not having them, they had reached their occupational ceilings early and now, at twenty-five, found them uncomfortably low.

The baffling question for the counselor, then, is how to help these boys and girls discover these facts while they are still in school, so that they may develop the motivation to acquire an education which will equip them to deal with that abstraction called change. The important questions for the curriculum maker are the nature and the essence of the experience leading to the motivation to learn these skills, and how this essential experience may be incorporated into the high school curriculum.

## IV. Guidance for Continuity

What I have said about discontinuity and irrelevance for some should not cause us to lose sight of the problems of continuity and relevance for others. There are still, and will continue to be, stable and conventional careers; there are now many, and will increasingly be more, youths to whom high school seems relevant and for whom progressive careers are challenging.

Vocational guidance needs to give these young people a clearer idea of vocational life stages; it needs to help them use the resources of the school and of the community to develop sound and realistic self and occupational concepts; it needs to give them knowledge of and skill in the use of the techniques of exploration and establishment; it needs to help them to enjoy and to grow with the excitement of intellectual discovery, esthetic appreciation and creativity, and social service. The school plays an ever-larger role in making these experiences not only available, but of avail.

## THE CHALLENGE OF HIGH SCHOOL FOR SOME OTHERS

The continuity of the careers of some, the accepted relevance of high school for many, and the stability and conventionality typical of the middle class should not be permitted to obscure the fact that education is for many pupils, and can be for many more, an intellectually, esthetically, and socially stimulating experience. That learning can be an exciting adventure is a truism so oft repeated that one is ashamed to state the very important fact. The recent interest in excellence in education has done a great deal to make school work and school experiences more challenging and more absorbing than ever. The current generation of college students, as shown in reports by Keniston[6] and others, is characterized by intellectual, esthetic, and social service interests and motivations which have rarely if ever been paralleled in our history. Our better high schools share in this ferment, and it seems likely that, as the current crop of college graduates moves in ever-greater numbers into high school teaching, more and more schools will share in it.

## V.  Implications for Guidance Practice

What methods, resources, and instruments are appearing today in the changing vocational guidance which I have been discussing?

1. In this age of automation, computers promise to have some impact on vocational guidance—perhaps we counselors are not as immune to obsolescence as I earlier suggested. At least eight projects are probing the possibilities of computerized educational and vocational exploration, individual appraisal, and counseling. Although the names and emphases of the various projects vary,

this is, in fact, what David Tiedeman at Harvard, John Cogswell at the System Development Corporation, John Flanagan at the American Institute for Research, Jo Ann Harris at Willowbrook High School, Joseph Impelliteri at Penn State, Murray Tondow at Palo Alto, Eugene Wilson at Interactive Learning Systems, and Frank Minor of IBM with Roger Myers and I at Columbia[7] are doing. None of us supposes that his equipment, his system, his program, will displace counselors; but there is no question but that we will produce methods and materials which will greatly modify the work of the counselor and greatly facilitate the processes of self, educational, and occupational exploration.

2. In this Great Society, recognition of the true meanings and implications of class differences will lead to the development and use of all-class, as contrasted with middle-class, vocational guidance practices. The usual concomitants and consequences of socioeconomic status will be taken into account in appraising aptitudes, interests, and motivation and in presenting and exploring educational and vocational information. Occupational analysis will be supplemented by career analysis. The probabilities of stable, conventional, unstable, and multiple-trial careers will be shared with students and clients; the characteristics of these careers, and their determinants, will be an integral part of career information; and possibilities and methods of shaping careers in terms of valued goals rather than in terms of traditional determinants, through the effective manipulation of social and educational resources, will be considered by students and counselors.

3. The new emphasis on bringing talents into contact with resources for their development and use will give new prominence to placement skills in counseling. Placement will be conceived of as more than merely getting a student into a suitable college (although this is beginning to be something of a feat) or into an appropriate job (another type of placement which will surely acquire new dignity); placement will increasingly be viewed as a bringing together of persons and opportunities for personal growth combined with the meeting of a social need. Placement will be a major instrument of

guidance, rather than its objective, whether the placement is in a class, a club, a part-time or vacation job, a college, an entry job, or a regular adult position.

4. The use of placement to further development will be one aspect of a developmental approach to vocational guidance in which counseling is continuous over a period of time rather than concentrated at one critical decision-making moment in a student's career. The counselor helps the student choose, obtain, use, and evaluate experiences which will contribute to his self-understanding, to his understanding of the world of work, and to the making of wise career decisions as these are called for by his progress through the educational system and on into business or industry.

5. A developmental approach to vocational guidance calls for the beginning of vocational and self-exploration long before the first clear decision points are reached, before the junior high school, in the elementary school. At this level vocational exploration is done, not through courses in occupations or careers, not through posters, pamphlets, or career days, but through regular instructional activities. In social studies, in English, in music, and in art, children learn how people live and work; they develop attitudes toward work; they come to see themselves as potential players of various work roles. In this way they lay a foundation of occupational information on which they can draw as decision points are reached. The lives of the assembly worker, the store clerk, and the economist are known to them, as are the things they do, and the ways in which they have prepared to do them. The student will still not be an ambulatory *Occupational Outlook Handbook,* but he will have an orientation to occupations and careers which will enable him to make good use of that tool and of the computer programs which will supplement it.

6. The automation of production, of distribution, and of some services, the prolongation of the prime of life, and the larger numbers of young people in our increasingly affluent society, will increase the tendency to prolong education. This will mean an increased challenge to make it meaningful to greater numbers

and varieties of students and an increased opportunity to use the high school years for exploratory, as contrasted with preparatory, purposes. There is already less pressure on counselors to speed up vocational choice-making in junior and senior high school, more opportunity to use those years for try-out purposes. The traditional distinction between individual appraisal and occupational information-giving will be less significant than it has been in the past, for the two processes, and with them vocational counseling, will be blended in the planning, use, and evaluation of appropriate sequential experiences.

## REFERENCES

1. D. C. Miller and W. H. Form, *Industrial Sociology,* New York: Harper, 1951.
2. D. E. Super, *The Psychology of Careers,* New York: Harper, 1957.
3. A. B. Hollingshead, *Elmtown's Youth,* New York: Wiley, 1949.
4. A. Davis, *Psychology of the Child in the Middle Class,* Pittsburgh: University of Pittsburgh Press, 1960.
5. W. L. Warner, M. Meeker, and K. Eels, *Social Class in America,* Chicago: Science Research Associates, 1949.
6. K. Keniston, *Uncommitted: Alienated Youth in American Society,* New York: Harcourt, Brace, and World, 1965.
7. These and other projects are described in R. E. Campbell, D. V. Tiedeman, and A. M. Martin, eds., *Systems Under Development for Vocational Guidance: A Report of Research Exchange Conference,* Columbus, Ohio: The Center for Vocational and Technical Education, Ohio State University, 1966.

# Administrative Theory: The Fumbled Torch

ANDREW W. HALPIN

A detailed case-history study of "administrative theory" shows a movement promoted and pushed to a premature and spurious "zenith." The movement, representing an honest attempt to induce constructive innovations in one segment of education, has not produced enough second and third generation students and disinterested researchers. The danger here is that as writers write to a market, researchers will research to the market of funds available—one tends to submit proposals to where the money is. The danger, too, is one of promoters who force researchers into a stance of premature and often unjustified dogmatism. We need to protect those men who seek to understand and help education disinterestedly, and who would prefer not being associated with any movement or program.

Since the end of World War II, the graduate training programs in educational administration in this country and in Canada have gone through a period of profound and often disruptive change.[1] Many more students have been trained; an increasing number of students of high intellectual caliber have been attracted to the field of educational administration; the training, at least at a few major universities, has become dramatically less provincial and insular; and the students, for the most part, have become excited by a host of insights derived from the behavioral sciences. However, although these changes have had a significant impact upon both practitioners of administration and professors of administration alike, this impact has been more pervasive and more enduring among the professors than among the practitioners themselves. As one might have expected, the coterie of professors who, at the outset, were most closely associated with changing the emphasis in the graduate program for training school administrators were quickly identified—not by themselves, of course, but by the "old guard" of that time—as members of the "New Movement" in educational administration. These men were not content with the orthodox curriculum and procedures for training administrators; these men had the courage to rock the boat of complacency; these men were mavericks.

Every new movement, whether in politics, in religion, or in education, needs a new flag, a new banner, or at a minimum, a new pennant. It needs a slogan, a new drum-roll that will rally the troops to action. For reasons far more fortuitous than many of us would like to admit, the slogan for the "New Movement" became "Administrative Theory." This slogan had several virtues: it was enticingly concise; it did not, indeed, violate the truth of the intentions of the leaders of the "New Movement," and it had a distinct charismatic appeal.

The slogan did serve a purpose. The topic of "Administrative Theory" was added to courses in administration, and in several instances a course by this title was taught. Several books appeared with the slogan, or a closely related concept, in their titles.[2] Indeed, in November 1957, several of my colleagues at the University of Chicago and I organized a conference entitled *Administrative Theory in Education.*[3] A book published as recently as 1966 bears the title, *Theory and Research in Administration.*[4] Yet as one reviewer justly states, the book is about administration but does not deal directly with the heart of administration.[5] The critic, Professor James Thompson, could have been less kind; he could have noted that the book does not present even a single theory of administration in education. I cannot be that kind toward the author; the book does not present a single theory of administration in education, simply because there is no theory worthy of the name available to report at the present time. And even last week I finished teaching a course at the University of Georgia that is entitled "Basic Theories of Administration." I assuaged my conscience by conceding that this was a course title that was already on the books and by telling myself, *sotto voce,* that any student who still expected a necessary relationship between the title and the content of a course in education was too innocent to belong in graduate school.

But something has happened to the bright, starry banner that had inspired so many of us in 1957. My paper at that conference in Chicago was entitled "The Development of Theory in Educational Administration."[6] If I were given a similar assignment today—and perhaps this paper represents just that—I would be more humble; I would be tempted to lengthen the title to "Toward the Development of Theory in Educational Administration: Maybe, Perhaps, and If—." Or to do what I have done here, to shorten it to read, "Administrative Theory: The Fumbled Torch."

Some owners of small foreign cars have difficulty in locating their cars in large parking lots, especially when the tiny creatures get lost among the chromey monsters that reflect not alone the sun, but also the affluence that comes to men who are smart enough to be practical, to know where the money is. Prudently, the owners of the sports cars sometimes attach a large, bright artificial flower to the top of a tall radio antenna. The flower helps the owner find his car. Likewise, I now no longer look for the starry banner around which the groups of the "New Movement" had hoped to congregate. I am willing to settle for a fake flower, if it will at least help me locate a "car" that is not a fake.

Chronologically, we can divide the life span of the "New Movement" to date into three periods. Obviously, all chronological classifications are arbitrary; social and historical change never takes place along a clean-cut line of either development or decay. Thus, when I use dates as pegs, please recognize with me that each date has a probable error of perhaps two or three years and that the dates by which we peg any given phase of social change do not apply to this same phase for all parts of the country or for all universities, even within the same region of the country. With the aforesaid qualifications, I now use my pegs to demarcate the following three periods: 1947 to 1954; 1954 to 1964; and 1964 to 1969.

Furthermore, each man must write from his own place in time and with his knees bogged down in the quagmire of his own personal biases. I am no exception: I pretend to no false, aseptic objectivity. Rather do I lean toward the epistemological views of Michael Polyani.[7] Moreover, I can view the scene in educational administration only from the present point in time: May 1969. I have not yet lived into 1970 or 1975.

I will treat my topic in a somewhat off-beat fashion. First, I will describe how the "New Movement" developed historically. Second, I will summarize a few substantive achievements of this movement. Third, I will note why I believe that the promise of the movement has remained unfulfilled, and why the movement seems to have lost its initial, happy momentum. Fourth, and most importantly, I will examine the "New Movement," not in respect to its substantive achievement, and not in terms of its hopes, intentions and disappointments, but rather as one case-history example of an earnest but aborted attempt at innovation in education. Perhaps we can all learn from this case history, and from this experience, a few things that we should *not* do when we seek to induce change within any segment of the complex social system that we call American Education.

First, then, how did the "New Movement" develop? During World War II the graduate schools of America were depleted; young men were busy elsewhere. But population pressures had not ceased; new cohorts of children were headed inexorably toward the public schools, and the need for a rapid expansion of school facilities was flagrantly evident. And new facilities meant that a new corps of administrators had to be recruited and trained. Fortunately, a group of professors of educational administration banded themselves into an informal organization known as the National Conference of Professors of Educational Administration—the NCPEA. They held their first meeting in 1947 at Endicott, New York. These men recognized several shortcomings in the then current methods of training administrators. The courses at that time were essentially how-to-do-it affairs. Many of the professors in the field were ex-superintendents of schools who, it would seem, had chosen the professorship as a form of early retirement. Instruction was based upon neither theory nor empirical research. The case-study method of instruction had not yet filtered out of the schools of business administration into departments of educational administration. The professors therefore regaled their protégés with their own personal experiences as school administrators. We witnessed, to a discomforting degree, instruction by anecdote, often given by men in their anecdotage. Few of the professors at that time had had substantive training in the behavioral sciences, and their research techniques were, with rare exceptions, rather primitive. Nor were many of these professors even remotely aware of relevant research in the area of business administration, and, more particularly, aware of the vital research that had been done before World War II by Elton Mayo and his colleagues at the Harvard Graduate School of Business Administration.[8]

The mavericks who founded the NCPEA knew that something was wrong with their discipline of study. They knew that their field needed expansion and support, and they also sensed that to continue to expand their programs with just "more of the same" would not be enough. But here let me note quickly that the members of the NCPEA were a very small minority among the professors of educational administration in America; they scarcely represented what was going on in the field as a whole.

At about this same time, the American Association of School Administrators (AASA) became interested in securing financial support for graduate training programs in educational administration. The leaders of the AASA and the leaders in the NCPEA had a great stroke of luck for, during that very period, the Kellogg Foundation was exploring the idea of extending its support into new areas. The dialogue among the representatives of the Kellogg Foundation, the AASA, and the NCPEA resulted, in about 1950, in the Kellogg Foundation's decision to provide support for a research and development program in educational administration. This program, the Cooperative Program in Educational Administration (CPEA), sponsored and supported CPEA Centers at eight universities.[9] At some centers this support continued for ten years. The Kellogg Foundation was exceptionally generous in its funding—the total given was about $6,000,000— and was amazingly astute in providing supervision of the CPEA program that was both permissive and liberating. However, when the funding was phased out (about 1960-1962), only one of the universities at which the eight centers were located continued to support, financially, a comparable research effort in educational administration.

In 1956, the University Council for Educational Administration (UCEA) was established. The membership of this organization was composed not of individuals, but of member institutions committed to the support of quality research in educational administration. The first national seminar for professors of educational administration, sponsored jointly by the UCEA and the University of Chicago, was held at the University of Chicago in November 1957; its topic was: *Administrative Theory in Education.*

Perhaps the single most important date in the history of the "New Movement" is August 1954, when the annual meeting of the NCPEA was held at Denver. At that meeting the first "real" confrontation between behavioral scientists and professors of educational administration took place. Coladarci (of Stanford), Getzels (of Chicago), and Halpin (then at the Ohio State University) pointed out to the group—and not gently—that what the CPEA Centers and the members of the NCPEA were doing in the name of research was distinctly a-theoretical in character and sloppy in quality.[10] The reception that these three behavioral scientists received at that meeting can scarcely be described as cordial. A second important event took place at that same meeting. The NCPEA, with the financial support of the Kellogg Foundation, sponsored the book, *Administrative Behavior in Education,*[11] and elected as the editors Campbell and Gregg. Significantly, this book contained one chapter, by Griffiths, entitled "Toward A Theory of Administrative Behavior."[12] Furthermore, for the first time in a book on educational administration, a chapter written by a behavioral scientist was included.[13]

Thus, the first of the three periods that I have demarcated.

One of the eight CPEA Centers had, from the very outset, stressed theory-oriented research in the field of educational administration. This, of course, was not accidental. The Department of Education at the University of Chicago had had a long tradition of respect for scholarship and research. Professor Francis Chase, the first Director of the Midwest Administration Center (and later, before he became Professor Emeritus, Dean of the School of Education) vigorously supported this tradition. Happily, in 1951, Professor Jacob W. Getzels, who had taken his doctorate at Harvard and had studied with Talcott Parsons, had joined the faculty of the University of Chicago. In 1952, Getzels had published the earliest statement in which a plea was made to study educational administration within a psycho-sociological framework.[14] Even then, Getzels had stressed the need for theory-oriented research. At Chicago, Getzels, working with Egon Guba (at first his student, and later his colleague), developed a theoretical model for the analysis of administration as a social process.[15] Although his model was first reported in a publication in 1957,[16] Getzels and Guba[17] had earlier (1954) tested the model empirically, and Getzels' students, Ferneau[18] and Moyer,[19] had also tested the model empirically. Thus, from the very beginning, the program of the Midwest Administration Center was strengthened immeasurably by the fact that Getzels and Guba worked closely with the doctoral students in educational administration. Then, in 1957, Campbell became director of the Midwest Administration Center, and Halpin also joined the Center's staff. So, by a set of fortuitous circumstances, several of the more vocal spokesmen for the "New Movement" found themselves working under the same roof at Judd Hall. At that time there were, of course, other spokesmen—notably Daniel Griffiths, then at Teachers College, Columbia University (now Dean of the School of Education at New York University), and, among the younger men, W. W. Charters, Jr., then at the University of Illinois. But the point that cannot be sloughed off, and the one that I want to emphasize, is that from 1954 to 1959 an appreciable number of the men engaged in theoretically-oriented research in administration were physically centered at one spot. As I hope to note later, this circumstance was, paradoxically, both good and bad.

Now, what did the leaders of the "New Movement" emphasize? In short, three things:

1. That the role of theory be recognized and that "nakedly empirical research" be rejected in favor of hypothetico-deductive research rooted in theory.

2. That educational administration not be viewed provincially, and especially as distinct from other kinds of administration. That administration, as administration, without adjectival qualifiers, is a proper subject for study and research.

3. That, because education can be construed best as a social system, educational administration must, in turn, draw heavily from insights furnished by the behavioral sciences.

In retrospect, these three recommendations certainly do not appear momentous. Yet the very fact that these three objectives had to be declared speaks eloquently about what had been "the state of the art" in educational administration prior to 1954.

So much for the historical background for the present analysis.

And now, to my second question: What are a few of the substantive achievements of the "New Movement?" By substantive achievements I mean major research contributions, contributions which, for the most part, have opened new conceptual vistas and have been generative of fresh testable hypotheses. I will cite five studies and will present them in order of their publication. All five of these studies were done during the second of the three periods that I demarcated earlier: 1954-1964.

First is Halpin's study, *The Leadership Behavior of School Superintendents;* this research was done in 1954, and the findings were published in 1956.[20] He used the Leadership Behavior Description Questionnaire (LBDQ) which had been developed by members of the Personnel Research Board at The Ohio State University in earlier studies of the leadership behavior of aircraft commanders. By factorial methods, two dimensions of leadership behavior had been identified: consideration and initiating structure-in-interaction.[21] Halpin[22] and Hemphill[23] had both shown that "effective" leadership behavior is associated with high scores —as determined by the group members' descriptions of their respective leaders—on both dimensions. In the study of superintendents, Halpin had fifty superintendents describe their own behavior on the LBDQ, had the same superintendents described on the same instrument by a sample of their teachers and also by the members of their respective Boards of Education. He found that the members of the different Boards agreed among themselves in their descriptions of their respective superintendents, and that the different faculties also agreed among themselves in the descriptions of their respective superintendents, but that the descriptions by the Board members, by the staffs, and by the superintendents themselves did not yield high correlations with each other. He noted that "democratic administration" was not an especially useful concept, that this concept did more to muddy our thinking and our acting about leadership than to clarify it. School administrators tended to perceive consideration and initiating structure as antithetical behaviors, and what they believed to be "democratic administration" turned out to be behavior high in consideration but low in initiating structure, behavior which the empirical evidence shows to be associated with *ineffective* leadership. The empirical findings of this study and of related studies were less important than their effect in opening the path for a fresh conceptualization of leadership behavior, especially in respect to the consideration and initiating structure dimensions of behavior.

The second study was that by Getzels and Guba, published in 1957.[24] Using role theory, Getzels and Guba developed a model of administration as a social process and posited two major dimensions of behavior in this respect: the nomothetic dimension and the ideographic dimension. The major strength of this model is that it interlocks both psychological and sociological constructs into a schema from which fruitful, testable hypotheses have been derived.

The third study is the most monumental single study ever conducted within the field of educational administration. *Administrative Performance and Personality*,[25] by Hemphill, Griffiths, and Fredericksen, was published in 1962 and is an intensive study of the personality characteristics and the administrative performance of a sample of 232 elementary school principals. These principals were subjected to a highly sophisticated and realistic set of simulated experiences in which they performed tasks demanded of principals in their day-to-day job. This is not the time to report the detailed findings of the study, but simply to cite a few major accomplishments of this comprehensive study.

First, the on-the-job behavior of the principals was factor-analyzed, and a set of useful dimensions were identified, along with techniques for measuring a principal's behavior on these dimensions. Second, it was shown that different principals could be characterized by different, highly specialized administrative styles, that these styles could be identified and measured, and that the relevance of each style to the task of a specific principal-ship could be adjudged. One very practical outcome of the study was that the simulation technique, used originally for research purposes, was later modified for use as an extremely powerful device for the pre-service and the in-service training of elementary school principals. At both the theoretical and the practical levels, one other finding and observation stands out clearly: that the principals' scores on their simulation experiences provide a more useful and a more meaningful set of criteria for judging the administrative performance of these principals than do some of the traditional measures which heretofore had been used as alleged criteria. Among the dubious criteria to which I refer, to be more specific, are ratings of principals by their superintendents.

The fourth study, *Executive Succession and Organizational Change*,[26] published in 1961, is by Richard Carlson. Carlson studied a sample of recently appointed school superintendents and compared those who had been appointed from within the school system with those who had been appointed from outside the particular system. In short, this is a comparison between "the locals" and "the cosmopolitans," between those superintendents who are place-bound (i.e. geographically) and those who are career-bound—that is, oriented to their profession rather than to a geographic location. Carlson then shows "how and why" the career-bound executives are in a better position than the place-bound executives to effect organizational change.

The fifth study is Halpin and Croft's analysis, *The Organizational Climate of Schools*, first released as an Office of Education report in 1962, and later published in 1963.[27] These investigators constructed a sixty-four-item Organizational Climate Description Questionnaire (OCDQ) which they administered to the teachers and principals of seventy-one elementary schools. By factorial methods they identified eight subtests and six organizational climates. The six climates are posited along a rough continuum running from the "open" climate at one end to the "closed" climate at the other. One important contribution of this study is that it provides a way of conceptualizing the organizational climate of a school. Over and over again, the concept of "morale" has been used sloppily, and although much research has consistently shown that "morale" is not an unidimensional construct, many educators have persisted in behaving as if it were. "Organizational climate" is a more useful concept than "morale" if for no other reason than that it forces us "to think multidimensionally." The OCDQ has been used as a basis for self-evaluation programs in schools, and the findings for a specific sample of schools have been used in "administrator clinics." Although more than 150 studies with the OCDQ have been reported since 1963, and although this technique has been used extensively in the United States, in Canada, and in Australia, a great amount of further basic research with the instrument is sorely needed.

This organizational climate concept appears to have an especial relevance to the problem of change and innovation in educational practices. One can hypothesize that a school with an open organizational climate will—as compared with a closed climate school—be more receptive to change and innovation. Indeed, the OCDQ would appear to provide a useful technique for the differential diagnosis of schools with respect to their receptivity to change. In a recent paper, *Change and Organizational Climate*,[28] Halpin has discussed certain aspects of this issue.

Here, then, are five types of studies that characterize research within the "New Movement." Of course, there have been other studies, but most of them have been derivative. But these five, none of which is derivative, represent the temper of recent research in educational administration. Three of the five studies— those done by Halpin, by Hemphill and his colleagues, and by Halpin and Croft—raise serious questions about the uncritical use of current criteria for recruiting, selecting, and training school administrators. And what impact have these warnings had? Very little. These investigators can rightly feel that their findings have been "blowing in the wind."

When I am forced, as I am now, to look back at the substantive research achievements in educational administration since 1954, I find that I am not impressed. Certainly in 1954 I had hoped for greater progress than I later found in 1964. Yet the hope for the "New Movement" and the excitement about it did reach a peak between 1954 and 1964. The heady fragrance of great promise was in the air.

I have chosen 1964 as the date for the end of the second period (1954-1964) for one other reason. In that year, Griffiths edited the NSSE yearbook, *Behavioral Science and Educational Administration*.[29] This book accurately depicted the "state of the art" in 1964, one decade after the Denver meeting of 1954. In reviewing this book[30] in 1965, I noted my impression that the movement had begun to run down. My impression on this score has not changed in the past four years; indeed, in my view the period since 1964 has been anticlimactic.

Thus far, I first have summarized the development of the "New Movement" and, second, have described briefly—with respect to specific studies—five substantive achievements. As I have indicated earlier my remaining comments will be directed, third, to why I believe that the promise of the "New Movement" has not been fulfilled, why it has lost its initial happy momentum, and fourth, to what we can learn from this experience when we view it as one case-history example of an earnest attempt at innovation in education.

Third, then, why has the movement begun to run down?

One reason is because the *idea* of administrative theory was, in the first instance, oversold. Because many of us had expected too much, too quickly, and too easily, we foredoomed ourselves to discouragement.

I now quote from comments I wrote in 1957.

> In the world of everyday affairs we are all barraged by appeals to change to something new, appeals often bolstered by the argument that the new is more scientific. This applies to detergents, automobiles, and movements in education. For example, there is a tendency in education to latch onto new movements not so much because of their intrinsic soundness,

but simply because they are new. "Progressive" education, the look-and-say method of teaching reading, and group dynamics have all been embraced with greater enthusiasm than understanding. Fads and styles in education, like the length of women's skirts, have had their ups and downs and have been pursued accordingly. We would like to hope that our pursuit of theory in educational administration is based upon appeals of less transitory revelation. Our task deserves a stronger commitment than this.

Some of us will need to examine our motives rather carefully. Are we seeking a better *understanding* of theory, or are we trying to *promote* the idea of theory? These motives are starkly different. In seeking a better understanding of theory, and through patient application to the development of better theory, we shall gain greater acceptance for this approach. But this acceptance will come about through the merit of what we actually accomplish, not through claims of what we intend to accomplish. Neither a particular theory nor the *idea of theory* are things to be sold, to be marketed as an advertiser might market a new breakfast cereal.

Most administrators develop skillful techniques to secure support for the programs they initiate; this often is necessary in education, and for this reason some promotional ability on the part of the administrator is useful. But because these promotional skills have proven effective in other areas, a few of us may be tempted to apply them to the present endeavor. This would be a mistake, would reflect motives alien to our purpose. Our gains must be measured by the integrity of the ideas we generate, not by the number of supporters we enlist.[31]

At that time in 1957, I scarcely realized how closely I had fitted myself into the cloak of Cassandra. In brief, what I predicted then has unfortunately come to pass. The original statements about the role of theory in administration and about the importance of theory-oriented research had been made by behavioral scientists who had spoken from their own direct experience with research. But the second wave, and the subsequent ripples of writings on this topic, were set into motion by authors who did not have the same depth of direct experience with research. Some of these popularizers seized upon the idea of "administrative theory" and made it into a slogan. A few of these men wrote more than they knew. Yet they were safe, because their readers knew even less.

But please note the difference between the behavior of the popularizers—the men who saw "administrative theory" as a good bandwagon to ride—and the men who stuck to their benches and produced research. Consider the men associated with the five studies that I have cited earlier—Getzels, Guba, Carlson, Hemphill, and Halpin: in none of their research studies do these men indulge themselves in "intellectual games" about administrative theory. They simply do research and report what they find. Where their ideas have been *promoted*, they have been promoted, not by the research investigators themselves, but by other professors whose forte is promotion.

The promoters quickly become infatuated with the sound of their own words. They talk themselves into their own belief in "instant change." And when this change is not as instantaneous as they would like, they become disillusioned and move on to another new movement upon which they can exert afresh their promotional skills. This is not surprising; throughout history there have always been some men who enjoy changing mistresses in mid-dream.

In brief, the promoters, other men of action, and the "True Believers" whom Eric Hoffer[32] describes are temperamentally entirely different kinds of men than those whose primary devotion is to research.

I think that there is a lesson in this experience for those of us concerned with any "New Movement"—or innovation—in education. The lesson is simple: avoid the Madison Avenue approach. Keep the promoters out and do not make rash promises. Yet, even now, as I look at the panoply of education programs sponsored by "The Great Society," I hear the hollow noises of the pitchmen, and I hear many promises that scarcely can be fulfilled. Indeed, in the handling of the Negro problem and of the more general problem of the culturally deprived, we can already see examples of the boomerang effect that comes from sudden and sobering disillusionment on the part of the recipients of the promised benefits. Teddy Roosevelt told us to speak softly and carry a big stick. Likewise, I would suggest that we in education learn how to promise less and deliver more.

There are other reasons why the "New Movement" has slowed down. One clue to these reasons is provided by Van Miller, the recently appointed editor of the *Educational Administration Quarterly,* a journal sponsored by the UCEA which began publication in 1965. This *Quarterly* is designed to provide a forum for discussion and dialogue among professors, social scientists, and graduate students in the field of educational administration and research-oriented practitioners. Miller, in the spring of 1967, after paying his tribute to Roald Campbell for his contributions as editor during the *Quarterly's* first two years, then noted:

> Throughout the years when a journal of this sort was being proposed, it was easy to get the impression that a great backlog of worthy articles awaited such a channel and that a large number of able writers had only held their talent in check because the appropriate vehicle was not available. The impression thus gained and the actuality of having an adequate supply of publishable manuscripts in hand are two quite different matters.[33]

Miller acknowledged Campbell's success in attracting manuscripts and added:

> Then, as now, the generation of a sufficient number of quality manuscripts was the primary problem in getting out the *Quarterly.*[34]

He ended with a plea:

> People throughout the field are urged to scout out those who have ideas and material appropriate for *Quarterly* articles and to encourage them to submit manuscripts for consideration.[35]

Can one readily see the editors of the several American Psychological Association's journals, or of major journals in the field of

Guidance and Personnel, making a similar plea? The APA journals, for example, are usually flooded with good manuscripts from which the editors can make a selection, and the authors of even top-notch manuscripts sometimes have to endure a publication lag of as much as two years.

I would note, too, that proposals submitted to the Office of Education for research in the area of educational administration have been conspicuously weak. And the bulk of doctoral dissertations that appear in this field lack sophistication with respect to research methodology.

In view of the fact that our hope for progress was so high in 1957, what has happened to bring about the present conditions?

The answer, I believe, is frightfully simple: we have had no talent *in depth*. Men such as Getzels, Guba, Hemphill, and Halpin—for example—did not train enough doctoral students with research strength *and* an interest in administration to replace even their own numbers, let alone to provide professors for counterpart posts at the many American universities where doctoral programs in educational administration are conducted. I am not faulting these men for this; the reasons are complex and reside in the strange subculture of educational administration as a profession, and the research men themselves are, indeed, not responsible for what happened. To put it bluntly: not enough fresh research talent was attracted to the field, and too few of the men who were attracted had sufficient respect for craftsmanship. To be sure, there were exceptions, notably Professor James Lipham, at Wisconsin, and Professor W. W. Charters, at Oregon. But on the whole, what we soon discovered was that there was no fresh blood in Transylvania.

I mentioned earlier that, of the eight CPEA Centers, the one which had most emphatically stressed theory-oriented research was the University of Chicago. And I noted that in 1957 many of the vocal spokesmen of the "New Movement" were physically under the same roof. I said that this was good *and* bad. Why it was good is obvious. It was bad because, even with the massive Kellogg Foundation support given to all eight Centers, the talent available, even then, was not equally distributed geographically. In terms of the critical-mass analogy, things probably had to work out as they did at Chicago. Scholars need to be where they have other scholars with whom to talk. But the problem to which we have not found an answer is this: Having established a critical mass at one university, how do we keep it "critical" there and, at the same time, gradually establish similar critical masses at other institutions? Obviously, without sufficient depth of talent, and without continuous development of new talent, the task cannot be achieved. This problem, of course, is not confined to the field of educational administration.

I may add, parenthetically, that this identical issue applies to the present network of Regional Educational Laboratories and Research and Development Centers. These programs have sprung forth like Minerva from the head of the Office of Education. And they were established when there already was a dearth of research talent even at the major universities. As a result, we have witnessed in the past few years a nationwide game of musical chairs, highly seasoned with a few acts of flagrant piracy. Perhaps a few of the Regional Laboratories will succeed in building up for themselves the necessary critical mass of talent, but I doubt very much that all of the Laboratories and all of the R & D Centers can succeed on this score. When you spread talent too thinly, you may get activity, but I am not convinced that you get productivity.

But to come back to the field of educational administration, I need to make a few other observations. I look at a group of men who, either as professors or as students, have been associated with the Midwest Administration Center within the past ten years. These are all men who understand research and also understand administration. Five of these men, to cite a conspicuous example, now are Deans at Chicago, Stanford, Wisconsin, Utah, and Ohio State. I reveal no state secret when I say that the deanship is literally a killing job and that the exigencies of the job make it difficult, if not impossible, for a dean to maintain his scholarly and research interests while also fulfilling his responsibilities as a dean. These men must make choices and must make these choices in the light of the expectations imposed upon them by others with respect to their own professional roles. Thus, these five men have been lost to the "New Movement" because, in one sense, they have become victims of their own success. And consider, too, what has happened to an organization such as the Midwest Administration Center. Within the past five years it has had three different directors.

And what has happened to the research men from the halcyon period? Their own interests have taken them into fields other than administration or to jobs where they function, primarily, as research administrators.

And where are the critical masses in graduate research in administration today? One hope is the R & D Center at the University of Oregon where Carlson, Charters, and Hills are colleagues. Nor has Chicago entirely lost its power. But, in looking across the country today, it is difficult to say, "Here is a university that offers an outstanding graduate program in educational administration and that also puts a strong emphasis upon theory-oriented research."

And this brings me back to the title of my paper: *Administrative Theory: The Fumbled Torch.* In the fifth century B.C., the Olympic Games in Greece included a torch race. The torch not only represented the fire of Prometheus, but also symbolized the knowledge of man. The race was a relay in which each runner, in turn, passed the torch to the next man. During the period from 1954 to 1964, several of us who participated in the "New Movement" in educational administration carried torches that burned with a bright and fervent flame. But as the race continued, few of us found another runner to whom we could pass the torch. In short, the torch has been fumbled, and there it lies on the ground in the middle of the arena.

I find this situation ironical. The promise of the "New Movement" is not a hollow one. There is much important research to be done; there are many able men to be recruited and trained; there are imaginative training programs to be developed. What is needed is a university center where, with respect to educational administration, the excitement of the period from 1957 to 1962 can be re-created: but, without fanfare, without promotional gimmicks, and in a fashion that will permit the sponsors to profit from the experience that I have discussed here. Yet the torch still lies there on the ground, and I don't see the eager hand of any university reaching out to grasp it.

True, the UCEA is still operating and recently has embarked upon an international exchange program in educational administration. True, the R & D Center at Oregon is operating. Yet, my general impression is that the momentum of the original movement has been drastically diminished.

So much, then, for my discussion of the emphasis upon administrative theory as a major aspect of the "New Movement" in educational administration.

And now to my fourth and final point. What, if anything, can we, as educators, learn from this experience? The movement has represented, and even now represents, an honest endeavor to induce change and to introduce constructive innovations in one segment of the complex social system that we call American Education. Yet, honest and good intentions do not appear to be enough. And what frightens me is that I see analogous movements in other segments of education: for example, the push for compensatory education and the development of programs for the culturally deprived; the attempt by the network of Regional Educational Laboratories to produce "research packages" that will then be adopted by schools in the field—or perhaps, engineered into these schools; the emphasis, by Bruner and his colleagues, on learning as an act of discovery.[36] I become concerned because I discern the strong likelihood that some of these "pushes"—even as the administrative theory movement in educational administration—will become victims of sudden abortion. Elsewhere, I have discussed a few of the conditions that induce such abortions.[37]

In education we are all trying to do so much. Nor can we complain about a lack of financial support; the U. S. Office of Education has opened a cornucopia from which all blessings seem to flow. But the distribution of this largess seems to be based upon four tacit assumptions:

1. That planned change can be engineered, and engineered on a big scale and a long-range one.
2. That change can be effected quickly and, indeed, dramatically.
3. That money will buy anything.
4. That noble intentions and hard work, especially when coupled with enough money, will achieve the results that we desire.

These four assumptions are extremely comforting, and extremely American. This is not the place to discuss the current "Mythology of Change"; I have done that elsewhere.[38]

Moreover, nowhere do I see an explicit recognition that there probably are not present within the educational establishment today enough people with the necessary talent and skills needed to man the host of programs that are being generated. Nor is this dearth of talent confined to the educational establishment. A similar shortage is found in the medical and nursing professions. And our American corporations, despite the financial incentives they offer, continue to encounter severe shortages of the necessary talent and skills required to keep the machine going. Furthermore, each of these segments of our society is competing for the same brains. And very simply, there just are not enough brains to go around.

But my passion has driven me to the brink of besmirching myself with clichés, and I could be only too easily tempted into belaboring the cheap and the obvious. What, in my story of the fumbled torch disturbs me so much? I cannot stop the rise and fall of fads in education. I cannot make the operators cease and desist. I cannot stop men from writing to a market and from striking the market while it is hot. I know that when one theme or fad has been used up, another will take its place. Right now, in administration, there is a great stress on the value of "systems theory." And this idea, too, will run its course. But I surmise that the less that this idea—or any other idea—is promoted, and the less that it is made the victim of organized promotion, the longer will interest in the idea be likely to survive.

Thomas Griffith, in his stimulating book, *The Waist-High Culture,* describes one aspect of the problem that plagues us. His examples pertain to the popular arts, but apply, I fear, equally well to what we do in certain of our professions.

> Considering the nature of their work, most people feel rushed. Creativity itself in such a climate must account for its time, and often cannot wait on inspiration but must adapt what is close to hand. We thus tend to take a decorator's interest in other cultures—ransacking museums or far-off places for combinations of colors or design motifs we can borrow from them—and no wonder that we "use up" these other cultures so fast and move on to something new. Fashion can never stay long enough to discover what a culture was really about, but moves on restlessly like one of those crop-picking machines that whooshes across an entire field, gathering in its claws all that it can profitably pick up and leaving behind what would have been uneconomic to pause over. This year a Polynesian theme; next year the Etruscans. The present temper of the arts, to satisfy people's longing for something more than the bleak and efficient functionalism of our uncrafted homes and offices, runs toward diluted borrowings (simplified Victorian, etc.). The designer's task, in adapting a past elegance, is to see that what is intricate be made simple, or capable of easy reproduction, for we no longer have time to be original or thorough: we adapt, we imitate and we multiply, and are becoming a society of tomb robbers.

And in a footnote to this passage, Griffith adds:

> And since our pace is what it is, we then have soda fountains, which are another form of profitable approximation: we must have speed and therefore accept clutter; we demand economy and must tolerate crowding and rapidity of turnover. Drugstore counters are a hurried substitute for restaurants, and the American, understanding their function, puts up with their annoyances. While a counterman slops an egg into a pan and whips up some ready-made tuna mash, an adman—at a low unit cost—has been at work on the menus, spreading his crispy crunchy promises that have no relation to what will be de-

livered; for it is the American custom never to acknowledge a lowering of standards in service or product, but to deny stoutly that anything has been lost along with what has been gained.[39]

I can see the crop-picking machine whooshing across other fields. In the name of the practical, in the name of developing packages of research products, I hear the Regional Educational Laboratory programs as they now whoosh across the field of education.

And the policy decision of pouring Office of Education funds into applied research has brought with it the announced and practical policy of giving little support for basic research in education. Obviously, he who controls the funds determines what research will be conducted. And many young and ambitious professors fall into the trap. They submit proposals according to where the money is. They propose, if you will, to a market.

Now, I do not say that the Regional Laboratory program will not produce some good, practical, and useful products for public education. Nor do I doubt that some of these products will be disseminated and used intelligently in our schools. My doubts and questions are of a different order. First, I question how durable or stable the program can be. There are built-in features that will tend to induce high personnel turnover. Specifically, I doubt that all of the Regional Laboratories that are in business today will still be in business next year. And properly so! I also expect to see a great amount of wastage. For every X amount of useful products, I would expect to see YX amounts of trivia. I will not place a value on quantity Y, but I suspect that it could run rather high. Now, I know the counter-argument. The problem of inducing massive change in American Education will be likened to getting men on the beach at Normandy: if you get 5 per cent of the troops on the beach you are ahead of the game. The analogy is a dramatic one, but I do not think that it applies to the induction of social change. In brief, I am wary of crash programs of any kind and of anything that bears the touch of the operators.

I have discussed the case-history of "administrative theory" in educational administration in detail, hoping to point out that the very acts that we committed in an effort to promote the movement pushed it to a premature and spurious "zenith" and that now, as a stockbroker would say, "A correction has set in." But if, when a correction sets in, a stock has not already built a firm base and has not already come into firm hands, the stock invites massive bear raids and is defenseless against them.

I have already described how several substantive research contributions to the "New Movement" were made by men who were not promoters or operators; men who, while functioning as scientists, simply stuck to their benches, without engaging in disquisitions about the nature of theory or the nature of research. One other point has to be made about these men. They were not interested in practical results, they were not interested in research products, they did not care whether their findings were disseminated or not. *In a genuine sense these men were disinterested.*

Strangely enough, this very point reveals what bothers me most about the operators and the promoters. Rather than being disinterested, they are *too much interested.* They literally have too much at stake, they have invested too much personal prestige and status in their efforts. And, having too much at stake, they cannot afford the luxury of the three most indispensable qualities or attitudes required of a scientist: tentativeness, dispassionate inquiry, and patience. The operators and the planners are forced, instead, into a stance of premature and often unjustified dogmatism.

I am not saying that the planners can avoid this dogmatic stance; indeed, to be decisive and to get things done in a world of action, the role of The Operator or of The Planner imposes upon them the expectation that they will be dogmatic. Moreover, strong social sanction is given to this particular type of dogmatism.

I have no illusions. We will not stop the crash programs. The temper of our times is such that we probably will generate more and more crash programs, each with greater aspirations and perhaps greater desperations than the one before it. I see the juggernaut, and I am even reconciled to it.

For what then do I plead? And what specific lesson do I see in the case-history of the "New Movement" in administration? What do I learn from it that I think can help us behave more wisely in planning for the future of American Education? What I conclude is, I fear, almost platitudinous. Certainly, the idea I offer is not new and is perhaps childlike in its innocence.

Simply, I would like to protect those men who seek to understand and help education *disinterestedly*, those men who prefer to stick to their benches away from the noise of the promoters and the operators, those men who would prefer not being associated with any movement or any *program*. I would like to see such men—and especially the younger among them—given both sanctuary and support. I do not pretend to know in what ratio funds should be allotted to A or to B, to the "too much interested" men as opposed to the "disinterested" ones. But intuitively I sense that a policy by any professional group, or worse yet, a policy construed as a national policy, that drives talent into A at the utter expense of B is an extremely short-sighted one.

Let me illustrate my point by a modern-day allusion to Noah's Ark. Suppose, to posit the most extreme instance, that the wise men of all nations saw as imminent, not a flood, but atomic disaster, and that they, in a desperate hope, decided to man an ark just on the off chance that those on the ark might survive to nourish a new Phoenix from the ashes of The Great Contretemps. (I am back, as you will note, to Thornton Wilder's *The Skin of Our Teeth*.) The wise men would have to choose the right mix for the passenger list. There would have to be women as well as men, otherwise the race could not survive. There would have to be men of brawn as well as men of mind; farmers, hunters, technicians, craftsmen, and in short, the minimum number of skills required for man's survival. I would like to hope that the wise men would include on their list men of thought as well as men of action; disinterested inquirers as well as interested doers.

In effect, this is what I am pleading for even now, while the need for the ark is, perhaps, not yet imminent. The Planners and The Operators may be right; I am willing to give them the benefit of the doubt. But even at Las Vegas I like to hedge my bets; I do not care to plunge all my bets on a single turn of the wheel, or on a single number. Likewise, I do not want to place all my bets on the dogmatism of The Planners; there is no guarantee that their plans will pay off. For this reason, I would like to see the bets on their success hedged. I would like to see some funds and some efforts provided for the nourishment of *the disinterested men.* Perhaps we may never need what these men have to offer. But, if a time should come when we, as a society, do need what these disinterested men can give, and if we should need—and, indeed, should need desperately—fresh, alternative courses of social action derived from sober reflection, I should hate to see us find ourselves in the awkward position of discovering that by then we, as a society, will have had already made these men extinct.

## REFERENCES

1. Currently these same changes are beginning to manifest themselves in Australia. *The Journal of Educational Administration,* edited by Professor William G. Walker at The University of New England, Armidale, N.S.W., Australia, reports and reflects these changes.
2. For example, Daniel E. Griffiths, *Administrative Theory,* New York: Appleton-Century-Crofts, 1959. Also Roald F. Campell and James M. Lipham, eds., *Administrative Theory as a Guide to Action,* Chicago: Midwest Administration Center, University of Chicago, 1960.
3. Andrew W. Halpin, ed., *Administrative Theory in Education,* New York: Macmillan, 1967; originally published by the Midwest Administration Center, University of Chicago, 1958.
4. Andrew W. Halpin, *Theory and Research in Administration,* New York: Macmillan, 1966.

5. James D. Thompson, "Review: *Theory and Research in Administration*, by Andrew W. Halpin," *Administrative Science Quarterly*, Vol. XI, No. 4, March 1967, pp. 691-694.
6. Andrew W. Halpin, "The Development of Theory in Educational Administration," Ch. I, *Administrative Theory in Education*.
7. Michael Polyani, *Personal Knowledge: Towards a Post-Critical Philosophy*, Chicago: University of Chicago Press, 1958.
8. For example, Elton Mayo, *The Social Problems of an Industrial Civilization*, Cambridge, Mass.: Graduate School of Business Administration, Harvard University, 1945. Also, Fritz J. Roethlisberger, *Management and Morale*, Cambridge, Mass.: Harvard University Press, 1941.
9. See Hollis A. Moore, Jr., *Studies in School Administration: A Report on the CPEA*, Washington, D.C.: American Association of School Administrators, 1957.
10. In response to their experience at the 1954 meeting, Arthur P. Coladarci and Jacob W. Getzels wrote their monograph, *The Use of Theory in Educational Administration*, Monograph No. 5, Stanford, Calif.: Stanford University School of Education, 1955.
11. Roald F. Campell and Russell T. Gregg, eds., *Administrative Behavior in Education*, New York: Harper, 1957.
12. Daniel E. Griffiths, "Toward a Theory of Administrative Behavior," *Administrative Behavior in Education*, pp. 354-390.
13. Andrew W. Halpin, "A Paradigm for Research on Administrator Behavior," *Administrative Behavior in Education*, pp. 155-199.
14. Jacob W. Getzels, "A Psycho-Sociological Framework for the Study of Educational Administration," *Harvard Educational Review*, Vol. XXII, Fall 1952, pp. 235-246.
15. Jacob W. Getzels, "Administration as a Social Process," in Andrew W. Halpin, ed., *Administrative Theory in Education*, pp. 150-165. A recent and further development of this theme is reported in Jacob W. Getzels, James M. Lipham, and Roald F. Campell, *Educational Administration as a Social Process*, New York: Harper & Row, 1968.
16. Jacob W. Getzels and Egon G. Guba, "Social Behavior and the Administrative Process," *School Review*, Vol. LXV, Winter 1957, pp. 423-441.
17. Jacob W. Getzels and Egon G. Guba, "Role, Role Conflict and Effectiveness: An Empirical Study," *American Sociological Review*, Vol. XIX, April 1954, pp. 164-175; "Role Conflict and Per-

sonality," *Journal of Personality,* Vol. XXIV, September 1955, pp. 74-85.

18. Elmer Ferneau, "Role Expectation in Consultations," unpublished Ph.D. dissertation, University of Chicago, 1954.

19. Donald C. Moyer, "Teachers' Attitudes toward Leadership as They Relate to Teacher Satisfaction," unpublished Ph.D. dissertation, University of Chicago, 1954.

20. Andrew W. Halpin, *The Leadership Behavior of School Superintendents,* Columbus, Ohio: College of Education, The Ohio State University, 1956; 2nd ed., Chicago: Midwest Administration Center, University of Chicago, 1959. An abridgment of this out-of-print work appears in Ch. III, of Andrew W. Halpin, *Theory and Research in Administration.*

21. Andrew W. Halpin, "The Leadership Behavior and Combat Performance of Airplane Commanders," *Journal of Abnormal and Social Psychology,* Vol. XLIX, January 1954, pp. 19-22.

22. Andrew W. Halpin, *Studies in Aircrew Composition: III The Combat Leader Behavior of B-29 Aircraft Commanders,* HFORL Memo. No. TN-54-7, Washington, D.C.: Human Factors Operations Research Laboratory, Bolling Air Force Base, September 1953.

23. John K. Hemphill, "Leadership Behavior Associated with the Administrative Reputation of College Departments," *The Journal of Educational Psychology,* Vol. XLVI, No. 7, November 1955, pp. 385-401.

24. Jacob W. Getzels and Egon G. Guba, "Social Behavior and the Administrative Process," op. cit.

25. John K. Hemphill, Daniel E. Griffiths, and Norman Fredericksen, *Administrative Performance and Personality,* New York: Bureau of Publications, Teachers College, Columbia University, 1962.

26. Richard O. Carlson, *Executive Succession and Organizational Change,* Chicago: Midwest Administration Center, University of Chicago, 1962.

27. Andrew W. Halpin and Don B. Croft, *The Organizational Climate of Schools,* Chicago: Midwest Administration Center, University of Chicago, 1963. An abridged version of this out-of-print work appears as Ch. IV of Halpin's *Theory and Research in Administration.*

28. Andrew W. Halpin, "Change and Organizational Climate," *Ontario Journal of Educational Research,* Vol. XIII, Spring 1966, pp.

229-247; republished in *The Journal of Educational Administration*, University of New England, Australia: Vol. V, No. I, May 1967, pp. 5-25.

29. Daniel E. Griffiths, ed., *Behavioral Science and Educational Administration*. The 63rd Yearbook of the Society for the Study of Education, Part II, Chicago: University of Chicago Press, 1964.

30. Andrew W. Halpin, "Essay Review: Behavioral Science and Educational Administration" (1964 N.S.S.E. Yearbook Part II), *Educational Administration Quarterly*, Vol. I, No. 1, Winter 1965, pp. 49-53.

31. Andrew W. Halpin, *Administrative Theory in Education*, pp. 13-15.

32. Eric Hoffer, *The True Believer*, New York: Harper, 1951.

33. Van Miller, "The Editor's Desk: A Tribute and A Challenge," *Educational Administration Quarterly*, Vol. III, No. 2, Spring 1967, p. 112.

34. Ibid. p. 112.

35. Ibid. p. 113.

36. Jerome S. Bruner, *On Knowing: Essays for the Left Hand*, Cambridge, Mass.: Belknap Press of Harvard University Press, 1962.

37. Andrew W. Halpin, "A Foggy View from Olympus," *The Journal of Educational Administration*, University of New England, Australia: in press.

38. Andrew W. Halpin, "The Mythology of Change," *Theory into Practice*, in press.

39. Thomas Griffith, *The Waist-High Culture*, New York: Harper, 1959, pp. 205-206.

# The Person and Organizations

> The aim of philosophy is sheer
> disclosure.
> The great difficulty of philosophy
> is the failure of language.[1]

We can define the person, or that self which is conscious of its deeper connections with human and cosmic life, as the latest product of the evolution from lower to higher stages of existence.

Conflict will exist, not only as a necessary evil, but as a condition of existence in the person, the group, and probably in the innermost structure of life. No human being becomes a person without inner conflict.

But whereas the isolated and ego-centered individualist destroys the community, the kind of individualist who is at the same time a person in the fullness of his self and the depth of his relations, is the architect of the true community.

## I. The Person

It was my original assignment to discuss the relation between the self and organizations. In the course of my considerations I found that in order to clarify the concept of self I would have to find a way through the linguistic labyrinth which is characteristic of both the common and the scholarly vocabulary we use for connoting the mysterious entity we call the human "self."

I am fully aware of the hazards of such an enterprise, for in the course of time a group of concepts has developed around the human person which are used in an entirely undifferentiated manner, sometimes as synonyms, though they are not strictly synonymous, and often merely as symbols of an entirely vague and evasive mental picture or of a perception that somewhere there is "somebody." In contrast to such hazy notions I wish to find out what we really mean when we address others and ourselves as beings endowed with a feeling of inner continuity and self-identity in the midst of a constantly changing world. And why, to ask another question, do we hesitate to attribute such terms as "self," "individual," or "person" to an animal?

The most comprehensive concept denoting an individual human being seems to me, for reasons which I will explain later, to be not the term "self," but the term "person," and that is why I have entitled this paper "The Person and Organizations" rather than "The Self and Organizations."

## A. THE I

In this connection I intend to discuss six interrelated concepts: namely, the concepts of I, ego, individual, self, person, and finally, mankind, or humanity.

The word which each busy human being uses probably a dozen or even a hundred times every day for indicating his presence in front of other persons—often also silently in front of himself—is the word "I." It is the most basic expression for distinguishing the self as a conscious individual from other I's or objects. It signifies the subject-object relation in our intercourse with the visible and invisible world and is, as such, the most fundamental and primary existential concept, mysterious and underivable from anything else, for without a perceiving and apperceiving I, human experience would be impossible.

Mostly, however, we are rather sloppy about the I. Only in moments of exposure, of self-assertion or of contradiction, does the word I receive its full weight.

In the phrase "I think" the word "I" has often only a very slight personal character. It could almost be replaced by such a phrase as "One thinks." Or while pointing at a tree, one may just as well say "There is a tree" instead of "I see a tree." Thus, "I" and "we" or "many" are often used interchangeably. Indeed, the existentialists (see Heidegger's untranslatable "Das Man") reproach us for being so deeply drowned in a conventional mass culture that it really would make no difference whether we said "I" or "everybody." The sense of authenticity, so the existentialists maintain, is lost. There is no self, no person, no sense of distinctiveness in the modern I.

Certainly, the submersion of the I in an ocean of anonymity is deplorable. But we should not forget that it is not merely a sign of self-surrender but a sign of health if we do not always take ourselves so "damn seriously," but feel, though unconsciously, an inner community with our neighbors and ultimately with all mankind. Actually, we would become insane if with every I we use we tended to emphasize our sense of existential separation from others.

However, even with humble members of humanity the importance of the I changes within different contexts. For instance, someone may *not* see the tree which I am seeing. Or he may *not* think as I expect him to think. Then I answer: "But *I* am seeing the tree," or "But *I* think so." Then the I changes from a mode of indifference to a mode of individualistic distinctiveness. It approaches the meaning of self, ("I, myself").

If we apply the foregoing reflections on the I to psychological cases, we may find a psychiatrist discovering a change in a patient when the latter pronounces the first personal pronoun I with a different intonation pattern. Needless to say, modern child psychology also has become interested in the infant's passage from just being in his world, or being himself the world, to his first expression of his identity, "Here I am." Or a teacher may discover that a hitherto indifferent pupil raises his hand and says, "Teacher, I do not believe it." This is a statement of beginning self-assurance which one might rarely, if ever, hear in schools belonging to an authoritarian culture. A good teacher, however, likes the disagreement because it indicates an element of individuality emerging from a so-far passive mind.

B. THE EGO

The second term related to the self-identity of a human being is the word "ego." Despite the amazing quality of the English language to absorb foreign words, the word "ego" still has a flavor of foreignness about it. Our dictionaries tell us that it did not appear in English literature until as late as about 1800. Indeed, ego reminds one today of psychoanalysis (the ego precariously balancing between the id and the superego). Also the words "egoism" and "egotism" come to one's mind; generally, these terms are used in a pejorative sense. But whatever the meaning in individual cases, mostly the concept of ego connotes the image of a human being in some isolation, no longer safely embedded in his society and in life as a whole.

C. THE INDIVIDUAL

When we speak of this or that ego, we always have in mind a specific "individual." Originally, the term meant an indivisible whole or a distinct entity separate from other beings. In that respect it is a somewhat emphatic form of I-ness. There are, however, shades of meaning to the term that reach deeply into the modes in which various cultures react to the eternal questions of man.

In a somewhat sweeping manner one could say that cultures which habitually and indiscriminately use the term "individual" reveal thereby an anthropocentric mentality, as manifested by the Greeks in contrast to the theocentric Babylonians and Egyptians. In England, so I gather from our etymological dictionaries, the word individual was rarely, if ever, used before the seventeenth century, or, in other words, not before the gradual change from a religious to a secular conception of the human person. And if we call someone an "individualist," we may allude to his originality and courage of independence. Even if he organizes a mass riot, we expect him to march at the head of the crowd or to direct the show of protest from some central office with telephones on his desk.

Generally, outspoken individualists are incapable of forming a community in the spiritual and moral sense of the term. For the execution of particular purposes they may form alliances, but these alliances will dissolve when they have fulfilled their objectives or when their failure becomes obvious. The German sociologist Ferdinand Tonnies would have said that individualists may form "Gesellschaften" (associations) but cannot join together in genuine "Gemeinschaften" (fellowship).[2]

Indeed, most nations have never, or have only lately, learned the art of genuinely cooperative or democratic living, or of combining individual liberty with loyalty to a greater whole. The French, while living under centralized absolutism, or the Italians and Germans enclosed in small feudal principalities, were for a long time deprived of the chance for democratic learning through active participation in political affairs. Thus they tended either to expect orders from above or to withdraw into themselves and to develop a form of private individualism which made them ill-fitted to form a united nation when the chance of self-government arose. The Germans in particular have continuously wavered between the two poles of excessive authoritarianism and excessive individualism. Thus they have been engaged in an endless search for national identity, embarrassing historians because the latter never knew whether they should characterize them as authoritarian or rebellious, obedient or refractory, conventional or critical to the degree of cynicism.

In contrast, the English, as a people with only brief periods of absolutism and with a great respect for the value of established custom, could afford a high degree of decentralization and have never needed as much legislation, bureaucracy, and coercion as most other nations. They knew that freedom requires agreement in the basic conditions of living together. Therefore they, like the Americans, could dare the risk of freedom.

Historically, individualism arose with the Renaissance when outstanding men severed themselves from collectively accepted

standards of living and thinking. Individualism has grown with
the protest of science, with the enlightenment and rationalism
which outmoded jaded feudal and religious forms of interpreting
the human being and his world, and finally with the modern
technical and competitive forms of business and production.
Here again we can observe the paradoxical interaction between
individualism and collectivism, for it is exactly the historical
movements just mentioned which have brought about mass
wars, massive nationalism, gigantic employer and labor organizations, and finally "the lonely crowd."

Probably the old farmer was, and so far as he exists still is,
more of an individualist with a strong insistence on independence
than millions of our city dwellers. But he did not feel himself
lonely or "alienated," because he believed himself to be in the
hands of an embracing force, whether it was nature or nature's
God, vast and immense, sometimes frightening, but always
near. On the other hand, one's neighbor in a modern apartment
is but an anonymous entity severed from other anonymous
entities by a number of thin, yet impenetrable walls.

## D. THE SELF

A human being with a strong dose of individuality is, so we
assume, one with a similarly developed sense of "self." We might
even suspect him of "selfishness" or "self-centeredness."

On the other hand, through the whole history of human
thought, the concept of self has also had a dimension of ethical
depth, often with metaphysical and ontological directions. Except in highly technical philosophical language no one speaks
of "I-hood" or of "ego-hood." But we speak of "selfhood" in the
sense of a productive form of self-identity and of self-respect,
without thinking of a narrow form of individualistic self-assertion.
If someone has "found himself," he has not been engaged in an act
of isolating himself from the rest of mankind. On the contrary, he
has found his self only because he has entered into a ground of
human existence where mutuality, love, and responsibility count
more than personal gain. To paraphrase a famous dictum of

Goethe: Only when the ego vanishes, does the deeper self appear.

Of course with these ideas of submersing oneself in the whole of being, we reach far beyond the limits of the discursive and empirical intellect into the realm of mystical religions. That does not mean, however, that thereby we transcend the possibility of human experience, for the inner relationship between "doing" and "becoming" is one of the most profound experiences of those men who have deepened our understanding of ourselves and our place in the cosmos.

To approach the problem of self from another angle, war is never a war among selves, but a fight between divided men. Nor is crime an act of selves, but of individuals who have lost their selves.

## E. THE PERSON

The fifth concept by dint of which the individual members of humanity indicate their identity is the concept of "person." *Persona,* as is well known, originally meant the mask of the actor in the ancient theater. In the course of time, the mask began to symbolize the character of the player. It became identical with a specific person, his appearance, his moods, and his role in life. I always feel something I may call eery in that process of transfer of the mask to the person behind it. Does it perhaps indicate that we all are actors, playing a role which we have not chosen ourselves, but to which we have been assigned by some unknown poet, the world poet or the creator, master of the tragedy as well as of the comedy of life? Indeed, in a deep sense we all are *personae dramatis,* appearing on the stage, taking our part in the acting, and disappearing from the proscenium into the unknown.

Some veil, some mask, remains about every human person, and wise men know that we should not too eagerly search for what is behind the appearance. We do not even know it with regard to ourselves; the claim to complete self-knowledge is a sign of stupidity. And nothing is more destructive to friendship and love than possessive and jealous inquisitiveness that cannot

bear the existence of the inner secrets of another person. Psycho- | ×
analysis, when practiced between lovers, means the death of love.

So what is a person? It is the synthesis, and at the same time
the greatest mystery of all, of the I, the ego, the individual, and
the self. Person is the self, in the deep sense of the word,
appearing in public, but never entirely open to the public.

In the Christian tradition, *persona* has a sacred meaning. It
is applied to the three modes of the divine being in the Godhead, or to Father, Son, and Holy Spirit, which together
constitute the Trinity. Also, Christ unites in his person his divine
and human nature. Thomas Aquinas uses the concept of *persona*,
in addition to the *personae* in the Godhead, also for high digni-
taries of the Church.[3]

According to the Catholic philosopher Jacques Maritain,[4] it is
through being a "person" that man can enter the Kingdom of
God, whereas as individuals we are tossed around by the waves
of desire and uncertainty. Therefore the person is sacred and
stands in the hierarchy of values above all earthly institutions,
even above the state.

NB

I do not know whether there exists a thorough study of the
process of what I may call the secularization of the concept of
the person. The various Oxford Dictionaries of the English
language tell us that in late Middle English a man or woman
of distinction was called a person. Then there must have occurred
that practice of expansion of titles of distinction to wider groups
of the population which is characteristic of recent times. Today,
e.g., everybody is called "Sir" who is relatively well dressed and
has white hair.

But we do not need to go back into history to appreciate the
significance of the concept of person. We can learn it from daily
experience. Even the most beautiful woman can become boring
to an educated man if she has no "personality," if there is no
spirit shining through her appearance. On the other hand, we
may feel strongly attracted to a man or woman whom the gods
have not blessed with beauty but with a rich inner life. We then
say: "I have met a real person." To speak in the language of the
painter, the concept of person suggests radiance, iridescence, or

translucency, whereas the concept of individual suggests opaqueness.


## F. HUMANITY

Our reflections on the nature of the person lead us to the over-arching concept of human selfhood, the concept of "humanity." Humanity should here be understood not as the mere sum total of all the mortals appearing on this earth and vanishing after a time, but in the sense of the Stoic-Ciceronian *humanitas,* which is somehow, though not totally, identical with the English "humanness" or the German "Menschlichkeit." All these concepts prove that man has regarded himself not merely as a physical creature, or as an isolated *individuum,* but as the carrier of a mission emerging within an evolutionary process from unconscious to conscious, and finally to self-critical and goal-setting forms of life. If the word "progress" had not been so completely secularized, as "national" or "economic" or "scientific" progress, it would be the right word in this connection.

All the great religions, though in mythical terms and still with an admixture of fear and superstition, express the conviction that humanity can rise beyond the desperate feeling of mere accidentalness and temporality and participate in a meaningful cosmic enterprise. In the history of secular philosophy, Hegel has powerfully expressed in his philosophy of history this self-persuasion of man. Mankind, so he asserts, is the instrument which the world spirit has chosen for its own self-realization.

Whatever the truth in these various intuitions, they are not mere fictions, but point at an inherent aspiration of man to attain selfhood, not merely personally, as previously defined, but collectively. All the thousand dreams about peace and cooperation among the nations of the world, stubbornly persisting in spite of war and hatred, are not merely expressions of the desire for a more secure and comfortable life. Rather they stem from the hope of man to create an order in which the self of a person can find strength and meaning. Every individual self desires to live in the embrace of a greater self.

To repeat, it is not merely universal peace that we want: this is an illusion anyhow. We want *wholeness*.

But with these considerations we have already passed to the realm of metaphysics. To a degree, one could use the concept of person as it prevails in a particular culture for the characterization of that culture's deeply underlying visions about man, life, and world.

It certainly is a reflection of profound trends in the Indian culture that some of its ancient speculative systems describe the I, or the self, or the person, as an organ of delusion. It takes Western men considerable time to project themselves into the consciousness of an Indian who speaks of the goal of the self as being to dissolve itself in the "Nothingness of Being." This is so, first, because they have to understand that for the Hindu and the Buddhist Nothingness is not merely a gaping void or a meaningless and incomprehensible concept, but the symbol of the creative abyss from which all life originates; second, because Western man is temperamentally unsuited for a passive conception of life. With few exceptions that come mainly from the mystical tradition, he regards the world as an arena where one either fights or loses. Also, our climate is impatient with the dawdler. Even Christianity, with all its emphasis on humility, believes that transcendental bliss can come only after a life of battling the thousands of temptations which the devil plants within and around us.

Idealism, moral and philosophical, and all those various movements which we classify as humanistic, are expressions of a will-oriented attitude toward life. In systematic form, this attitude has been emphatically demonstrated by the German Johann Gottlieb Fichte, according to whom the empirical self recognizes and fulfills itself in the absolute Self. This absolute Self represents the highest form of willing and expresses itself through a perpetual succession of intellectual acts, as they manifest themselves in the human being. Willing and acting (*Tathandlung*) are the root and essence of selfhood. The more I will, the more I can draw the great Self into my individual self and thus enter into the inner order of Being.

Not long after Fichte, who died in 1815, another German, with the pseudonym Stirner (Kaspar Schmidt), produced the most eccentric (one may call it pathological) expression of Western ego-centeredness in his book, *Der Einzige und sein Eigentum*.[5] (The best translation may be: "The I and what belongs to it.") His theory of solipsism of which, of course, he is not the only representative, maintains that the self, or the *ipse*, is the sole existing phenomenon of which one can be really aware. The *ipse*, or call it the ego, cannot know anything but itself and its own moods and modes of existence and is, therefore, responsible to nothing but to itself. We move here, on the one side, to anarchism, and on the other side into the neighborhood of Nietzsche's tragic "superman." For what else but tragic can be the fate of a human being who looks at the human community as being a mass of rabble held together by its herd instinct? Whereas in Fichte and the whole of idealistic and Christian thought the human being is an integral part of the totality of being, in other words, a "person" in the full sense of its meaning, in Stirner, Nietzsche, or, to go into poetry, in Verlaine (before his conversion), or in Baudelaire (*Fleurs du Mal*), the person has become severed from the encompassing all-ness. In other words, he becomes a lonely and roving individual, in spite of the various excitements and diversions he may encounter.

In this connection it is noteworthy that the only more recent philosophical movement of world-wide influence is the movement of existentialism. However different its various expressions, certainly such terms as anguish, loneliness, estrangement, or self-alienation appear again and again. The individual has lost his own self, because he is out of contact with the human community as well as with the universe which nourishes him and on which he depends. He is sick and aching like a limb that has been severed from the warmth and circulation of the whole body. If anything, the whole genesis and character of existentialism offers the justification for my distinction between the depth of self and person on the one hand and, on the other hand, of surface-ness (the term surface-ness is used to avoid the word "superficiality," for living *super faciem* can be a very serious and tragic situation unlike our modern use of the word "superficial").

Yet, it would be entirely wrong if we characterized the Western personalistic emphasis primarily with regard to its more or less esoteric speculations or its aberrations. Western personalistic *voluntarism** has proved itself as an historical force of the first order. Indeed, the people of the West were the ones who not only wanted to live *in* the world, but to *change* the world, through the application of science as much as through political planning. The most aggressive force in modern politics, Marxism, is essentially the outgrowth of a voluntaristic form of Western idealism. Although in protest against Western idealism, it nevertheless grew out of it, like a rebellious child trying to correct its parents.

I cannot enter here into the current discussion about the idealistic or anti-idealistic genesis of Marx's thought. Suffice it to say that he brought to its culmination a movement that had its origin in the Renaissance, the Reformation, and the Enlightenment. Instead of accepting the human situation as being a result of divine dispensation, he intended to abolish its injustices by dint of systematic planning. In comparison to his prophetic activism, the speculative voluntarism of a Fichte was but the enterprise of a lonely thinker. Marx appealed to the initiative of the masses. In order to end the exploitation and degradation of the human person that the masses suffered at the hands of the more fortunate few, he pointed at the strength the human person could develop by collectivistic action. "Workers of the world, unite!" Nobody, then, will be able to resist your force, and you will change the depersonalized society of capitalism into a society where persons will be able to realize their human destiny and dignity by working within and through the collective whole.

A highly voluntaristic tendency pervades also the movement of thought which is generally described as characteristic of the American mind, whatever that is. It is pragmatism, as expressed with particular vigor by John Dewey. The difference from Marx, however, is that Dewey sees the salvation not in the dictatorship

* Voluntarism: Any theory which perceives will to be the dominant factor in experience or in the constitution of the world.

of the proletariat, but in that mixture of individualism and collectivism we call democracy. Growth, experimenting and experiencing, trial and error, and progress as the result of rational willing are central concepts in his philosophy.

Unfortunately, Dewey, like Marx, never developed a full metaphysics of the human person. On the one hand, he professed his indebtedness to the great idealistic thinkers, especially Hegel; on the other hand, impressed by modern science and disappointed with the pseudo-idealism of his early teachers, he always shied away from any metaphysical *a priori,* though without it he could not explain how "experience," the term he used most frequently, can come about and with it "that intellectual correspondence of our ideas with realities that we call truth."[6]

This reluctance, or this identification of metaphysics with obsolete dogmatism, is unfortunate, because it has brought about an unnecessary break in the continuity of American philosophy. If during the years before, between, and after the two World Wars the American philosophers of pragmatism and education had not neglected Charles S. Pierce so much in favor of the early works of John Dewey, the American concept of democracy and the movement of progressive education would have been richer in content, more inclusive of the *philosophia perennis,* and consequently less dogmatic. But Dewey himself is not "Deweyism."[7] Essentially, he represents a cosmic humanism, with a strong emphasis on the capacity of the human will to change the world of man from a static into a dynamic and progressive enterprise.

Because of their experimental and voluntaristic conception of the human person and his society, in other words because of their conviction of the possibility of systematic planning, both Marxism and pragmatic democracy are not indigenous to the East. This fact explains the many calamities in the political life of so many struggling nations which try to adopt either communism or the American style of politics.

However, the tree of culture has many branches, and they often intertwine. The Japanese, for instance, are mostly Buddhists, but they are at the same time very pragmatic. Their leading philosophical writers, especially Kitaro Nishida,[8] attempt nothing less than a synthesis of Buddhism, German idealism, and American pragmatism. No doubt, with the influx of Western science and technology, the Asiatic concept of self and person will undergo further modifications. The process of reorientation, needless to add, will be particularly difficult in large parts of Africa where people still live in tribal situations. How can those non-Western cultures achieve within a few generations what we—let us be honest—have not yet fully achieved within a span of several centuries? Ancient superstitions and magic conceptions about the human person still reach deeply into our modern life. We all have been growing up in a multi-leveled society, and so will our children. For instance, neither in our professional life, nor in our sexual relations and our marriages have we fully solved the problem of the emancipation of women. How can those societies do it where daughters of mothers who still live in a kind of serfdom leave their homes to study medicine, or sociology, or education in Europe and the United States, and then return? In many cases we know what happens: either a swift relapse into the old conditions of communal life and marriage, or an heroic struggle, sustained only by the thought that they prepare a better life for their daughters and thereby also for the men of the next generation.

But whatever the various explanations and obscurities which man has developed about himself, every normal member of the human race is in one respect very similar to any other one. He wants to live a healthy and productive life, to create some satisfaction for himself and his neighbors, and in spite of all disappointments and detours he struggles nevertheless for some purpose and order within and around himself. Indeed, the great and so-called other worldly religions are the most sublimated expressions of man's thirst for happiness and belonging—if this thirst cannot be fulfilled here, then at least he is given the hope for another world.

Now, as we look back at our previous discussion we can define the person, or that self which is conscious of its deeper connections with human and cosmic life, as the latest product of the evolution from lower to higher stages of existence. The person is extremely functional, resilient and adaptable to new situations; at the same time it is extremely complex, complicated, and sensitive.

The human being is endowed with a miraculous brain and nervous system. He can express his sensations in signs; he can cry, sing, dance in mirth or trample the ground in fury, paint, build and plant, and maliciously destroy what he has built. He can form concepts that reach over into the vast universe and make some meaning out of it, though we cannot be sure whether our frail human reason can reach into the inner secrets of the world, or the *Ding an Sich*. But however narrow our limits in the eyes of the eternal, we can predict the movements of the stars, and we can have history and literature. The person cannot only express his prehensions and transform them into action, he can at the same time look critically at his feeling, thinking, and acting. He can transcend himself, and it is only through this act of self-transcendence that he discovers the depth of his self and becomes a person in the true sense of the term.

We may call a human being with an abnormally low intelligence an "individual" and give him an individual name, but he is not a self, or a person. He has, as it were, got stuck on his way toward humanity. Even a highly developed human being may have had his sense of self blocked by disadvantageous experiences; he is not, so we say, the person he could and should be. It is then the task of the guide, be it the parent, the teacher, or the psychologist, to remove the blocks, or the "complexes," so that he can restore the disturbed order in himself and his relations to the world.

## II. Organizations

When we now try to investigate the nature and conditions of the human person in relation to the organizations which surround it, we should first remember that the human person is itself an organization, though—and this makes a decisive difference—the only one which has a consciousness of itself. Nevertheless, it has one characteristic in common with every other organization of which we know: it can be truly understood only as a part of a larger organization. In complete isolation it is bound to perish.

It could not even begin to exist. Even a simple metal or wooden tool, so the physicists tell us, is a gathering place of forces by which it is ultimately connected with the greatest organization we know, namely Nature. The same is true of the human person. When its contact with nature is broken, it dies.

And the more subtle and self-conscious an organization or an organism is, especially during its growth, the greater is its dependence on the organizations which encompass it. The whole world could be described as an enormous process of involvement —which is merely another way of saying that the universe is one, or a "cosmos," which is the Greek word for "order."

But however much each person, physically and mentally, is elementally dependent on the spending forces of life as a whole, there are certain immediate forms of organization on which the development and welfare of the human person eminently depend. This dependence has, from my point of view, never been more cogently described than in Pestalozzi's *The Evening Hour of a Hermit.*[9]

Antiquated though this work of the eighteenth century is in style and certain sociological aspects, it still is the most remarkable prolegomenon to modern psychology and existentialism. That which Pestalozzi calls a person's "truth" is nothing else but what I have called the true self, or that inner essence of the person which constitutes his highest degree of self-awareness and self-direction. If we interpret Pestalozzi's essay freely, and at the same time in the light of his other writings, then the organization most necessary for the sound development of the nascent human organism is the family, represented in the initial stage mainly by the mother. Only when this seedbed of growth is taken care of can the infant finally become a person and merge productively into the widening orbits of social life, i.e., the community, the nation, and mankind as a whole being enriched by them and enriching them by his presence.

As a child of the eighteenth century, Pestalozzi could still believe in the restorative power of the family. However, he saw it increasingly menaced by the surrounding culture, which like Rousseau, he found utterly corrupt. Those in power, whether rich citizens or the innkeeper Pestalozzi described in "Leonard and

Gertrude,"[10] exploit their dependents; the Church is allied to the upper classes and teaches a meaningless dogma instead of helping the gospel of Christ to become reality. The schools, if and where they exist, impart useless knowledge, while the clear and concrete language of the people becomes diluted by the vague and irresponsible vocabulary of a flaccid and fatuous literature. (What would Pestalozzi have said about the linguistic techniques of Madison Avenue, and the fact that only a few of our schools dare fight the octopus of advertising?)

In our part of the world much, though by no means all, of the gruesome poverty and social injustice against which Pestalozzi protested is gone. Yet, I cannot read his works without being reminded that the deeper self in the human person, or his "truth," is today in some respects even more endangered than in the time of the great Swiss.

The calamitous discrepancy between more schooling and more affluence on the one hand and the waning of authentic forms of living on the other hand has often been deplored. But perhaps we are too pessimistic. Has life not always been a risk? God, or the gods, or the Creation, or whoever is responsible for the glorious mess of life, have never expected man to grow in an atmosphere of undisturbed moral and social progress. Whatever there is worthwhile in humanity is the result of tensions between forces we name good or evil, constructive or destructive, kind or hateful, wise or unwise, but which all together seem to fit into the cosmic scheme, the ultimate nature of which surpasses our understanding.

In reality, the human person and his society, though being organizations, are by no means mechanical structures the parts of which function smoothly in relation to each other and to the whole according to the rules of causality. Even the human body is not a Newtonian model; psychic and often unpredictable elements are constantly interacting with the physical ones. All we can hope for is that man's mental and physical qualities form a configuration in which the harmonizing powers are stronger than the centrifugal ones.

Conflict will exist, not only as a necessary evil, but as a condition of existence in the person, the group, and probably in the innermost structure of life. The art of dialectical logic, i.e., the endeavor to reconcile contrasts on a higher level of thought, is certainly not merely an esoteric philosophical exercise, but the attempt of searching minds to make manifest and at the same time to overcome the polarities which apparently inhere in all existence. No human being becomes a person without inner conflict. To be sure, the good life needs peace, some comfort, and security, but if it is only that, it will wither like a muscle without exercise. Or it will generate the very contrary of what it desires: first boredom and then rebellion against boredom. The welfare state is the greatest progress in the history of mankind when it is built on effort, justice, and mutual responsibility. But if it offers no challenge, it will create a spirit of smugness and passivity and become the greatest danger of advanced nations.

We have come to the end. We have tried to disentangle the various highly undifferentiated connotations by which our conventional language characterizes the individual human being. We have set the self and the person, to a degree also the I, against the ego and the individual. The latter designate the human being in the state of isolation, the former suggest a stage of inner achievement in which man is aware of his belonging to ever greater social and cosmic orbits.

Consequently, every activity that has to do with the guidance of individuals—such as education, administration, and politics in the widest sense of the term—in other words with the life of men within the community and the world, cannot merely promote individualism.

Of course, every educational activity must be interested in the self-realization of the single person, or his "individuality," for a society that fails to cultivate such individuality degenerates into the inertia of conformism. But whereas the isolated and ego-centered individualist destroys the community, the kind of individualist who is at the same time a person in the fullness of his self and the depth of his relations is the architect of the true community. He saves it from stagnation as much as from the hysterical convulsions which characterize a mass society.

One brief word will best describe the relation between the person and the world of organizations: "interdependence." Without persons horizontally related to mankind, as well as vertically oriented toward values that make communities out of fighting crowds, human organizations lose their life blood. Nor will men who see the essence of life in "peace of mind" at all costs ever contribute to a sound organizational life.

What we as administrators, teachers, and guidance workers have to achieve is the art of politics in the profoundest sense of the term, i.e., the art of changing tensions, as they inevitably exist in the human and natural world, from futile frictions into rich forms of personal and cooperative living.

## REFERENCES

1. Alfred North Whitehead, *Modes of Thought;* six lectures delivered at Wellesley College, Massachusetts, and two lectures at the University of Chicago, New York: Macmillan, 1938, p. 67.
2. Ferdinand Tonnies, *Gemeinschaft und Gesellschaft; grundbegriffe der reinen soziologie,* Leipzig: Buske, 1935.
3. See Thomas Schuetz, *Thomas Lexikon,* Paderborn: Schoeningh, 1895, p. 592.
4. Jacques Maritain, *La Personne, et le Bien Commun,* Paris: Desclee de Brouwer, 1947.
5. Johann Kaspar Schmidt, *Der Einzige und sein Eigentum,* von Max Stirner (pseud.), Leipzig: O. Wigand, 1845.
6. John Dewey, *A Common Faith,* New Haven: Yale University Press, 1934, p. 44. See also p. 47.
7. Robert Ulich, *History of Educational Thought,* New York: American Book Company, 1945, pp. 315-336.
8. Kitaro Nishida, *Intelligibility and the Philosophy of Nothingness; Three Philosophical Essays,* Tokyo: Maruzen, 1958.
9. Partly translated by Robert Ulich. Robert Ulich, ed., *Three Thousand Years of Educational Wisdom; Selections from Great Documents,* Cambridge: Harvard University Press, 1950, pp. 480-485.
10. Ibid. pp. 485-507.